The Standard Book of Noun-Verb Exhibition Grammar

Niekolaas Johannes Lekkerkerk

Onomatopee 141

The Standard Book of Noun-Verb Exhibition Grammar

Niekolaas Johannes Lekkerkerk

Onomatopee 141

Table of Contents

Note to the Reader

It is my great pleasure to entrust you with this publication that is set among the codified microcosmos of the exhibition and its inhabitants, a volume which casts the exhibition as a space that is highly written, edited, and marked by discourse. The process of making exhibitions involves a hyper-formalist and spatial language that we, as curators and artists, employ but do not quite recognize or fully understand, even though we grapple with its material and discursive formulations constantly. At the same time, we appear unable to access the objects by which we "write" exhibitions, and through which we are enabled to shape perception. Here I am referring to a type of object we could call an "exhibition entity": an object that is not granted the status of being an art object, and one that is often referred to as a "support structure" that is at best an invisibly charged utilitarian object—from plinth to monitor, from plant to temporary wall, from slide projector to a dog in the exhibition space. Instead of adhering to a schema of "business as usual" in respect to the assumed invisibility of these exhibition entities, I have employed this publication to unfold an exhibition complex through which these "unapparent," delicate, and subtle modes of being emerge.

This publication aims to animate, speculate, to tell things differently, to say something about these objects that are simultaneously—and already— their own subjects, to subjectify the exhibition and its populace (look where objectifying the world has got us). Not necessarily to inhabit these objects-turned-subjects, or to shroud them in additional layers of representational grammar, but rather to maximize a poetic resourcefulness that allows us to gradually move away from a system of display, toward its reinscription in the key of a politics of display that posits a pluralized perspective on what can be accounted for in addition to and outside of the binary dialectic between human and art object. These pages set about to conduct fieldwork and collect notes on the exhibition apparatus, to show that what revolves around, within, and beyond any given system, resolves to be just as serious and important as what that system aims to convey. Let us call it an exchange of perspectives that may prompt us to realize that—in times of ecological mutation and general instability—we must approach these modes of being differently, to trigger an alternative set of ideas concerning the exhibition.

This book puts forward an assembly of entries that are not necessarily to be read in a linear manner; they are to be encountered, instead, in the key of a meandering exhibition visit. The entries have been ordered alphabetically—in other words arbitrarily, as if these entities could possibly adhere to our linear schemes—and often tend to be short in nature. Navigating the entries will entail holding many points of view in suspension, embracing a certain margin of opaqueness, and maintaining an open-ended series of connections in order to free the exhibition entities from the page and, in some cases, the duties of communication altogether.

Throughout the publication, Tim Hollander's drawings accompany a selection of entries, and function as a parallel amplification of the text's limits, resonating with the signs, symbols, systems, and mental building blocks we may employ to "make sense" of an exhibition. Hollander's drawings make the exhibition's silent choreographies—like a floor plan or a guided-tour formation—the objects of interrogation, casting them as significant languages and social fabrics that underpin the exhibition's constructed nature.

I am grateful for Timotheus Vermeulen's contribution to this publication. His text presents insights into our tendency to endow the human figure with the capacity to be the basis of reconstruction. He introduces a number of different templates to confront us with this tendency and to extend our thinking elsewhere—from the language of dolphins, to buttons, to the idea of space as an open-ended script.

On the level of the texts' formation, the editors from Publication Services have aided me to rethink entries, to depart from their categorical biases, and to renegotiate the terms by which these things and actors are commonly as well as historically defined.

With graphic designer Sonia Dominguez, I have worked to devise this publication as a container that playfully subverts the aesthetic connotations and mechanisms of a grammar book—its rule sets, its urge to index—and to mold it in the key of a fictional field guide, subjective compendium, or wayward navigational tool.

From this collective effort, the publication you are now reading emerges as a fragmentary prism for an exhibition and its constituents, for those modes of being we thought to be able to go without.

Niekolaas Johannes Lekkerkerk

Ecologies of Existence: On Approaching Life from Within the Exhibitionary Complex

Prologue to the Exhibition

Upon arriving at an exhibition, we enter the loaded grounds of the exhibition space: a cultural field of inter-human energy exchange. A space charged with relations between different actors—artists, curators, staff members, and visitors, among others—each with their different aims, ambitions, and intentionalities, and what we might call objects of interrogation, reflection, and interaction that have been brought forward and put on display. As an exhibition visitor, we move around white spaces, we roam through repurposed grey warehouses, and wander in and out of black boxes to have a lived experience of and encounter with art objects. Using the cerebral and physical resources that we have at our disposal, we may find our vision altered in response to what we perceive. Accordingly, we make corrections to our assumptions, ideas, and thinking with the addition of new stories and perspectives previously unaccounted for. Here I speak of a desirable outcome for an exhibition.

At this point it would be worthwhile to make a small indentation in the ground that allows us to construct such a situation, which I have so far been doing from a purely anthropocentric perspective. That is to say, there is an inclination to think that an art object is supposed to exclusively serve something that is only completed through the active consideration of the human figure, and that it can acquire no function when it goes unseen. What status does the art object have without us humans? I opened this text with a description of the relationality between actors in an exhibition—between visitors and art objects—but would it be worthwhile to seek a different, multidimensional, and pluralized perspective, rather than maintain a binary dialectic between human and art object? By what means could we scale the exhibition format so as to be receptive to polyphonic assemblages, to bypass the commonly implied dichotomies and binaries of internal and external, nature and culture, human and non-human agency, and to look for lively, diversified scenarios for an exhibition that would postulate an equal footing for other modes of being in the world? I would posit that a rethinking of the exhibition as a medium with different formats is urgent and relevant, in order to consider the ways in which matters of concern are visualized and displayed, especially in times of increasing and ongoing human-driven ecological mutations, within a somewhat recently envisioned and highly speculative geological timeframe that is now titled by some as the "Anthropocene."[1] How can we start to think outside of the perpetual feedback loop of object-subject relations, on the level of the exhibition, especially at a time in which we have created too much world (culture) to continue to be ourselves?

So, how do we visualize matters of concern, from a curatorial perspective, and on the level of the exhibition as a medium? Here I would posit that what is at stake are questions of how and by what means we are enabled to think and conceive of the possibilities of life within the ruins of capitalism.[2] In this essay I would like to suggest some possibilities for going outside our cultural field while remaining firmly embedded within the cultivated environs of the exhibition space—as if it were an ecology turned inward—as a place where species meet, where ontological and epistemological registers clash, overlap, and contaminate each other, where the organic and inorganic exchange properties, qualities, and performances.

1
Geologists have begun to call our time the Anthropocene, the epoch in which human disturbance outranks other geological forces. For a discussion of the Anthropocene, see: McKenzie Wark, *Molecular Red* (New York: Verso Books, 2015); Bruno Latour, "Agency at the Time of the Anthropocene," *New Literary History* 45 (2014): 1–18; and Rory Rowan, "Extinction as Usual?: Geo-Social Futures and Left Optimism," *e-flux journal 56th Venice Biennale* (July 31, 2015), http://supercommunity.e-flux.com/texts/extinction-as-usual-geo-social-futures-and-left-optimism.

2
Here I am paraphrasing anthropologist Anna Lowenhaupt Tsing from her book: *The Mushroom at the End of the World: On the Possibility of Life in Capitalist Ruins* (Princeton and Oxford: Princeton University Press, 2015), 18–25.

From Matters of Fact to Matters of Concern

As curator and writer Vincent Normand argues in his text "The Eclipse of the Witness," the exhibition as a genre could be seen as a generic object of modernity: an apparatus for disseminating knowledge and displaying power that, from its early manifestation as the anatomic theater, the cabinet of curiosities, and The Great Exhibition of 1851, has effectively situated and granted license to the viewing body of the human as the central authenticating agent and locus.[3] In modernity's reformation of vision, the figuring capacities of the human body were granted the power of objectification, as Normand writes: "this scopic regime is typical of the modern dualism of subject and object, visually founded in the placement of a detached observer, a subject, at the apex of a perspectival cone whose sides lead to an infinity of objects against which the subject measures itself."[4]

This authenticating perspective, through which the human was thought to have become both *de facto* investigator and reasonable judge of a world of appearances and objects, has arguably paved the way for the human figure to make its retreat and withdraw from nature into culture. With the aid of a host of mechanical and mathematical instruments—of Cartesian logic—the "outside" world was measured and mediated, effectively and selectively channeled and distributed as sets of objective truths into a singular anthropocentric reality—what philosopher Alfred North Whitehead would call the "bifurcation of nature."[5]

In a world in which encounters based on the notion of a stable, objective backdrop have ceased to exist, by what means could we overcome the persisting modernist aspiration of implementing a symmetrical divide

3

Vincent Normand, "The Eclipse of the Witness: Natural Anatomy and the Scopic Regime of Modern Exhibition Machines," in *Ecologising Museums*, eds. L'Internationale Online and Sarah Werkmeister (L'Internationale Online, 2016), e-book, 91.

4

Ibid., 97.

5

"Bifurcation is what happens whenever we think the world is divided into two sets of things: one which is composed of the fundamental constituents of the universe—invisible to the eyes, known to science, yet real and valueless—and the other which is constituted of what the mind has to add to the basic building blocks of the world in order to make sense of them." From: Bruno Latour, "What is Given in Experience? A Review of Isabelle Stengers 'Penser avec Whitehead'," *Boundary 2* 32, no. 1 (Spring 2005): 222–37.

6

Bruno Latour, "Why Has Critique Run of out Steam? From Matters of Fact to Matters of Concern," *Critical Inquiry* 30 (Winter 2014): 232.

7

The term "exhibitionary complex" stems from the eponymous essay by sociologist Tony Bennett, first published in *new formations* 4 (Spring 1988). In his essay, Bennett discusses Michel Foucault's perspective on the institutional creation of knowledge and power, for which he draws a distinction between "institutions of confinement" such as prisons, asylums, and reformatories (which are Foucault's focus) and "institutions of exhibition" such as museums. Where Foucault identifies a society of surveillance (panopticon penitentiary), distinct from the society of spectacle found in antiquity (public floggings and executions), Bennett suggests that the two exist simultaneously: the self-disciplining nature which surveillance engenders is reinforced through the spectacle of exhibition, seeking to "transform that problem [of order] into one of culture" and thereby "winning hearts and minds as well as the disciplining and training of bodies." To illustrate this point, the author refers to Graeme Davison's description of the Crystal Palace: the Crystal Palace reversed the panoptical principle by fixing the eyes of the multitude upon an assemblage of glamorous commodities. The panopticon was designed so that everyone could be seen; the Crystal Palace was designed so that everyone could see.

between the human subject and the world of objects and non-humans? In his text "Why Has Critique Run out of Steam?" philosopher Bruno Latour makes a plea for moving from matters of fact to matters of concern:

> *While the Enlightenment profited largely from the disposition of a very powerful descriptive tool, that of matters of fact, which were excellent for debunking quite a lot of beliefs, powers, and illusions, it found itself totally disarmed once matters of fact, in turn, were eaten up by the same debunking impetus. After that, the lights of the Enlightenment were slowly turned off, and some sort of darkness appears to have fallen on campuses. My question is thus: Can we devise another powerful descriptive tool that deals this time with matters of concern and whose import then will no longer be to debunk but to protect and to care, as Donna Haraway would put it? Is it really possible to transform the critical urge in the ethos of someone who adds reality to matters of fact and not subtract reality? To put it another way, what's the difference between deconstruction and constructivism?[6]*

I hold the belief that the "exhibitionary complex" as we understand it today is still firmly embedded within the regime of "matters of fact"—the human as the measure of all things—and should instead be actualized to cope with the "matters of concern" we are currently facing.[7] This would involve a problematizing of the dialectics between human and art object, and a reinscribing of ourselves into the mesh of agencies and relations that the exhibition and its unstable surroundings put forward.

In the exhibition of contemporary art, we may still experience an (over-) indebtedness to modernist traditions: we come across homogeneous "viewing" spaces serving as the backdrop to a cognitive trading floor in which pictorial regimes and material volumes come to hinge on their translation into text and concept. In this binary dialectic, the artwork indeed and undoubtedly has agency, it undergoes trials, it elicits reactions, and it becomes describable. However, the dialectical process only seems to move one way since the human is not actively exchanging its figuration with the non-human art object—it only appears to be open to enquiry by means of passive observation and reflection. Here, for the sake of our argument, we must also seek to overcome the exhibition's persistent tendency to construct matters of fact—to posit an art object as something given, stable, autonomously static, and ready for deduction—partly by projecting objects of knowledge (labels, acts of description) onto ontological horizons. What we comprehend about the art object, through description and empirical analyses, is by no means an apprehension of the material-discursive nature and being of the art object itself. A first move in order to emphasize matters of concern would be to renegotiate our empirical space of encounter and not exclusively lead our interpretations back to the sole enrichment of the human mind, which often tries to make sense of things by claiming there is a mind knowing this world through objects of knowledge. Instead, we must employ our interpretative capacities to apply ourselves back to the world.

An initial way to move toward a more diversified and inclusive *exhibitionary* worldview would be to look further into the inner workings of the exhibition, to make its relations explicit. In order to set in motion a process of loosening thought from the constraints of the human, we must de-normalize what is held still and (not) presented to us. We must become hairsplitters and paranoid readers that are willing to move beyond the thinking and behavior that refuses to look deeper than the giveness of our actions and the appearance of things. In this newly established experiment we cannot simply pick and choose according to our preferences, since the humblest props now play a role, and there is no longer a distinction between things and the environment drawn around them. Foreground and background start to dissolve, and we must become open to encounters with all the inhabitants of the space left open between humans and what is deemed to be an art object. Soon we may realize that within an expanded field of exhibition entities, those elements present and mighty real, but not granted the status of art objects, have now become prominent actors as well: from the plinth to the exit sign, from the Hantarex monitor to the plant, from the press release to the set of headphones on a stool, from the invigilator to the fluorescent fixture, from the wall text to the projection booth, from the display vitrine to the wandering dog, from the wall label to the slide projector, from the socket to the sound shower, from sound spill to daylight, from a leak in the ceiling to a temporal wall, and so forth.

The exhibition space is indeed densely inhabited by entities that, were it not for rendering ourselves sensitive to them, would casually bypass our senses entirely, not only as enablers and supporters of art objects, but equally as subjects by and of themselves. We are obliged to read and face them on their own terms as actors with figurations, trajectories, and functions of their own. By engaging in a process of rendering ourselves sensitive to an extended field of exhibition entities, we might start to see that what revolves around, within, and beyond any art object, resolves to be just as serious and important as that which any given scopic scenario aims to convey.[8] This position enables us to engage in the politics of location via the politics of display: a process of consciousness-raising via the exhibition as a seemingly self-contained unit, toward a widening of the frame, a registering of—in the words of Latour—"more reality thanks to the use of a larger number of templates." He continues, "Pluralism is here understood not as a plurality of points of view on the same reality but as a multiplicity of types of agencies to register more reality—hence the phrase 'mode of existence.'"[9]

[8] A debate that media theorist Jussi Parikka has exemplified most eloquently in his book: *A Geology of Media* (Minneapolis and London: University of Minnesota Press, 2015).

[9] Bruno Latour, "How to Better Register the Agency of Things," in *The Tanner Lectures on Human Values 34* (Salt Lake City: The University of Utah Press, 2016), 97.

We are living in precarious times, in a world where entangled ways of living and collaborative survival become increasingly important—Tsing calls this "contamination as collaboration," the idea that we are enabled to

10

Tsing, *The Mushroom at the End of the World*, 27–8.

transform through encounter and active perception-making.[10] Could we envision the exhibition as a potent and viable ground for envisioning new collaborative patchworks?

From Fieldwork-Taking to Patchwork-Making

As discussed above, if the entities encountered in an exhibition—specifically those that are not granted the status of art object—are thought of as self-organizing and withdrawn, we are confronted with the problem of how we, as humans, could be enabled to think and act within multiple ontologies. As the exhibition is a field of constant becoming and renewal, we are entrusted with the task of seeking a metamorphic "subject" that is equally responsive and quick on its feet. I am thinking here of a human that is willing to speak and think from a decentralized and post-anthropocentric perspective, on the charged grounds of the exhibition amid a multitude of beings. We are obliged to think and to grapple with our surroundings, not from a perspective that fantasizes a relation between being and knowing, but rather in terms of the human body being immersed in radically immanent relations.[11] Philosopher Rosi Braidotti has written extensively about the idea that we not only think with our minds, but with and through our entire fleshed existences: that we simply cannot step outside the bodies that we inhabit—the limits of our skin also demarcating the limits of our perception.[12]

11

Timotheus Vermeulen, "Borrowed Energy," *frieze* (August 12, 2014), https://frieze.com/article/borrowed-energy.

12

See: Ibid.

On the level of the exhibition, this kind of human embodiment may be activated by engaging in processes of applied ontology: a relationship-oriented approach in the register of speech acts, of inviting, of sharing, of rendering oneself sensitive to the call and response from things, of attuning oneself to matters of concern. This effort of vocalizing relationships between human and non-human agents, both living and inert, would surely invoke a diplomatic stance that treads rather lightly since most of the things encountered in the space of an exhibition—art object or not—may be thought of as unresponsive to our calls given their apparent silence. However, simultaneously, we as humans may acknowledge the difference-making between entities that we conduct on our own behalf. This is precisely the point at which we should not instigate ourselves as arbiters of truthful meaning and unidirectional understanding, by adding additional mental building blocks, among free associations, but rather speculate on whether the thing encountered would have said exactly the same thing if we were to speak and understand the same language. This is also the point at which we should avoid a deconstructive rewording of the meanings and functionalities, and linguistic plays and private languages allocated to the entities we encounter, but instead extend our minds and apply our bodies to the world by means of establishing communities open to possible material, affective, and practical acts of "reworlding."[13]

To conclude with some matters of concern: in the midst of ecological mutations and devastations, the radical depletion of life forms, and the continuous extraction from the material registers of the Earth, we could employ the exhibition medium to devise what Latour calls "metamorphic zones," "where humans and non-humans keep exchanging their properties" so as to become "friends of interpretable objects"[14]—or what Tsing defines as "polyphonic assemblages," the gathering of various entities with their different rhythms, scales, and reaches.[15] Conveniently stable, safe, and comfortable as the confines of an exhibition may seem to be, we ought to use it as a space to think about the world that is actually lived by us. Here we might as well face the idea that the life force contained in the exhibition and its spaces can no longer be read without thinking through the porous walls of our institutions. We must go outside of culture by means of culture, using the exhibition as a place from which to depart and return. To see what subsisting and co-present passages we can provide for while learning to stay with the trouble.[16]

13 Donna Haraway, "Anthropocene, Capitalocene, Plantationocene, Chthulucene: Making Kin," *Environmental Humanities* 6 (2015).

14 Latour, "How to Better Register the Agency of Things," 96.

15 Tsing, *The Mushroom at the End of the World*, 27–8.

16 See: Donna Haraway, *Staying with the Trouble: Making Kin in the Chthulucene* (Durham and London: Duke University Press, 2016).

The Standard Book of Noun-Verb Exhibition Grammar

Index

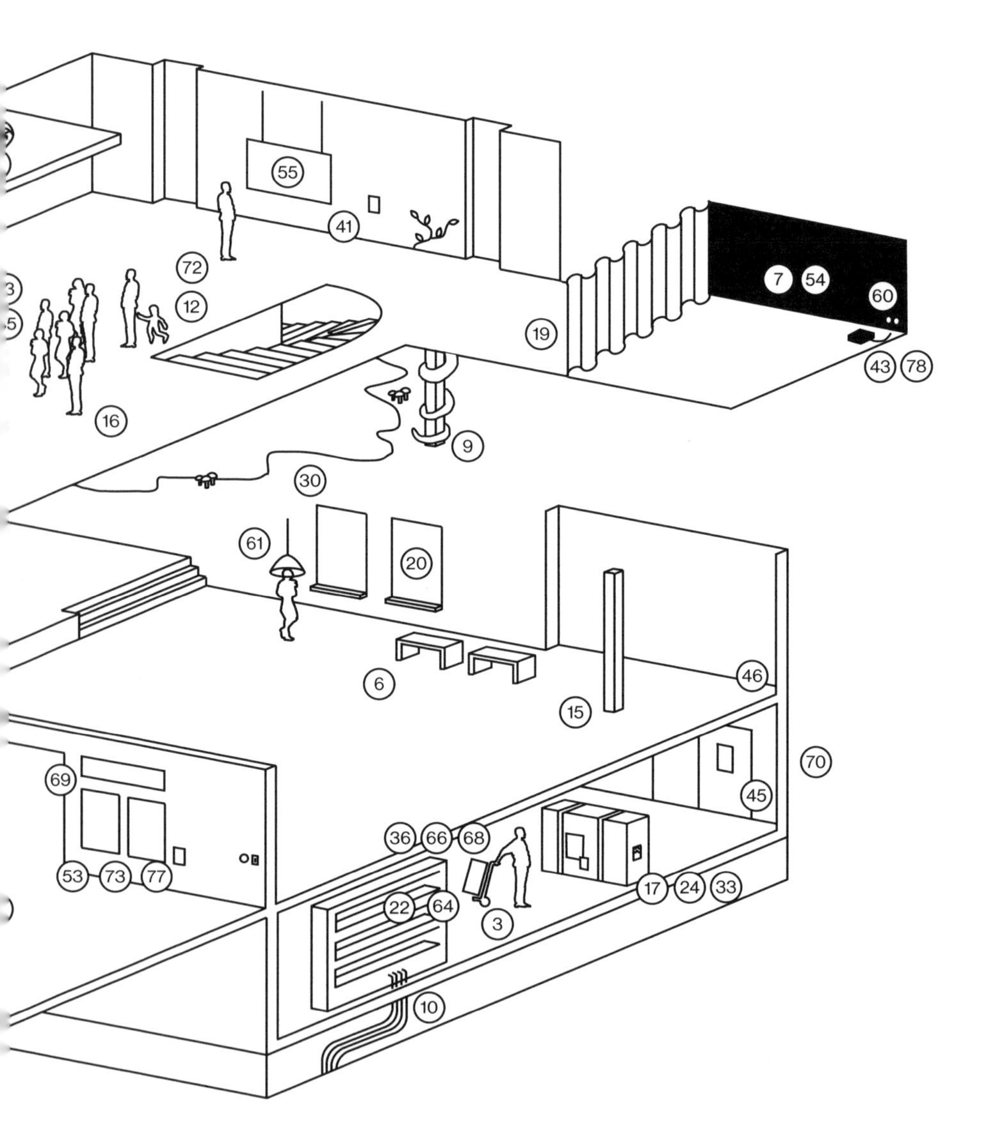

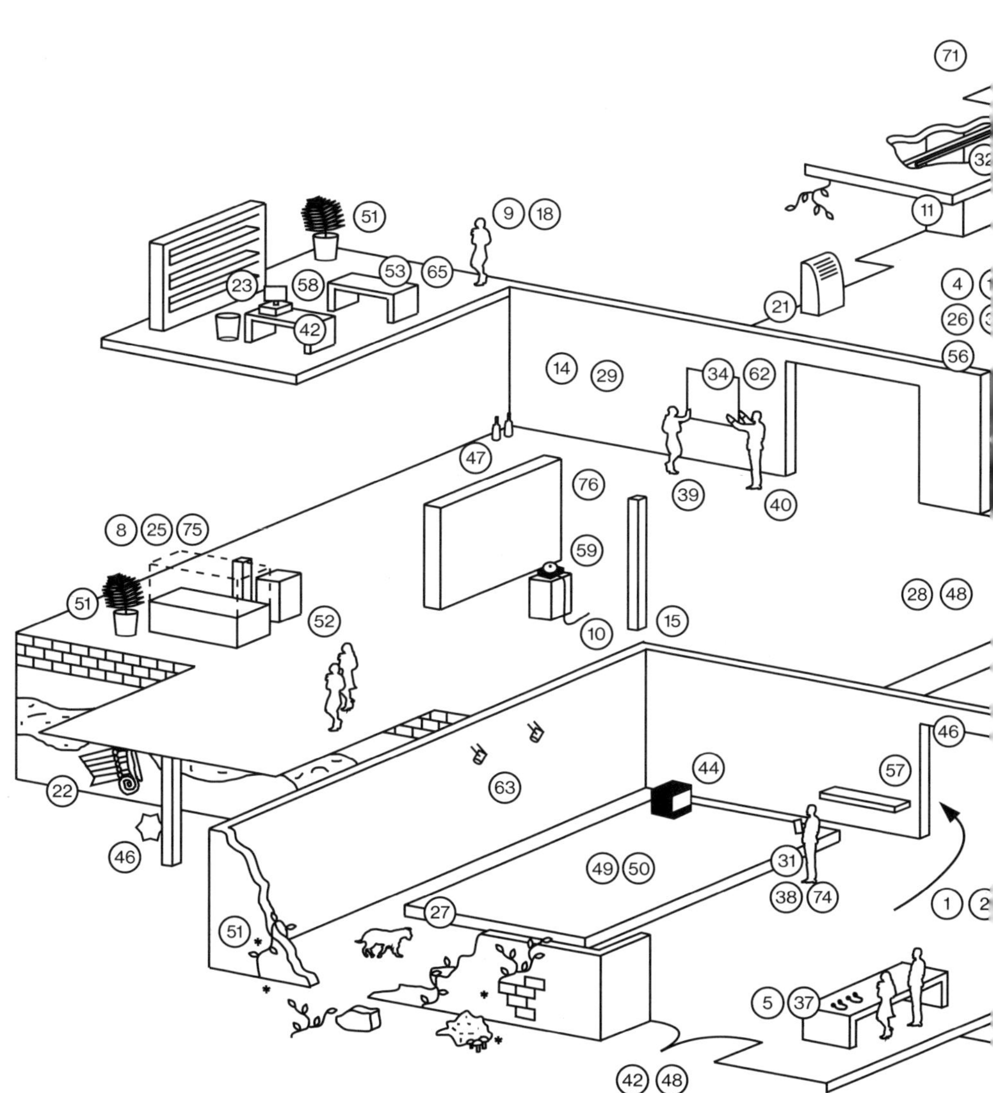

ACTING OUT

While pondering the potential of simultaneous occurrences within an exhibition, one could foresee the telling of many different stories, and plots and endings taking shape, especially considering the boundless but not necessarily infinite variables to be found in the interplay between x (texts) and y (actors). This is evidenced most clearly in the formation of a group exhibition, whose name is always legion, in which the joint standing and coalescing of displayed entities inform a potentially ever-increasing growth and accumulative sense of surplus value and excess thought.

Unlike film, where time is so often militantly moving forward, frame after frame, the space and time of an exhibition begs for an active stance on behalf of visitors, who are temporarily hosted figures with unscripted yet specified roles, roaming through the spaces of the exhibition in order to authorize and acknowledge what is on display. This support cast of exhibition visitors operates quite differently from extras on a film set, who move in and out of the frame as screen fillers or as the backdrop for an unfolding situation.[1] Essentially navigating on the axis of subjective knowledge and prior experience, with epistemological map in hand, the exhibition visitor seeks to allocate thoughts to physicalities and test the resonation of different ideas within the given frame of the exhibition. The realm of the exhibition visitor could also be described as a play within a play. Furthermore, if we temporarily disengage from the idea that exhibitions are solely developed for human visitors, we could argue that an exhibition in its final state, after having been brought to its desired shape by its producers, is positing a self-sustaining scene by way of its frame and its actors.

To roll out the idea of simultaneous time zones and spaces within a single exhibition frame is to posit a different textual and scenographic enterprise altogether. To do this, we must drift away from the stabilizing and pacifying way in which a gathering of multiple objects are made to adhere to and function under the encapsulating reign of a single overarching exhibition text—under which these gathered objects are so often subsumed.

The human visitor passes the entrance and faces two plinths, each holding a stack of room sheets printed on A4 paper. Still grappling with the idea of the double act, they enter an exhibition space where a substantial body of different works and objects are displayed. They take a copy of each room sheet and become acquainted with the checklists and floor plans printed on each. Things happen all at once, simultaneously and theatrically: some works appear on both sheets, others are detailed on only one. The realization that two (or more) exhibitions are being presented within a single hang and space is prompted, triggering a sudden perplexity and a gradual collapse of the visitor's perception, which is more accustomed to a group of works adhering exclusively to a single text. In turn, the constellation-upon-constellation of the various materials, texts, and objects is begging for closer inspection. Cross reading between the room sheets and the different frames they posit, they come to grasp a group of object-actors that are in no one's pocket, that instead find their inscription in multiple unfolding frames.[2]

1   Contrary examples include François Truffaut's *Day for Night* (1973) and John Smith's *The Girl Chewing Gum* (1976). In both cases, the director's script for guiding the extras is made integral to the film and the "mob" becomes subject instead of filler.

2   Curator Sam Korman once presented two exhibitions—entitled "June" and "Seagulls," at Simone Subal Gallery, New York, in June 2015—simultaneously and within a single hang, taking his cue from Anton Chekhov's play (and play within a play) *The Seagulls* (1896).

<table>
<tr><td>

②

ARROWS AND GUIDELINES

</td><td>

You are chronicling your way through an exhibition flooded with punctuation marks. Looking down, the floors are covered with lines and stripes, arrows and small printed footsteps, color-coded, it seems, and running in parallel. Here you might be reminded of

</td></tr>
</table>

grand thematic exhibitions that employ systems of reference and signification in order to usher visitors through certain artistic periods, biographies, and seemingly hermetic blocks of time. A form of crowd control, surely, but equally a means to bracket off and channel portions of information, to stretch and defer your possible anxiety that it would simply be impossible to overcome the sheer volume of material on view. An institutional arbiter of information distribution might hold the belief that regulating such lines of flight, with the goal of visitor control in mind, are a necessary means to general understanding, of being hospitable to a radical sense of understanding, even—an understanding that allows for no margin of vagueness or ambiguity on the level of the textual and spatial plotting of the exhibition's contents.

However, you are not in an exhibition with such a cohesive outline, nor have you been looking to settle for an "understanding" formed by connecting color-coded lines that shape a conveniently narrated, cookie-cutter experience. Instead, looking down at the ground, you are aiming at a different point altogether. You are on a search for the subtler accords that essentially constitute this system of guiding principles and coded linkages, determined to find out how it is able to communicate itself as a self-referencing structure rather than an aiding infrastructure. In order to come to grips with the routes presented, you have started to observe the different variations and patterns: red, yellow, green, and blue, and the small footprints. The latter seem to represent an even greater system of signification that bypasses your figuring capacities altogether. As the footprints lead quite haphazardly through the consecutive spaces, you suspect they are marking an infant's wander. Or, maybe they mark a route of exhibition highlights, as their chartered line seems rather brief and thus suitable for those more or less consciously desiring a streamlined narrative experience.

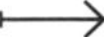

Artist (participating)	Critic	Pro
Artist (friend)	Cynic	Rookie
Artist (conceptual)	Dog	Sculpture
- a walk of 82 steps		
Artist (other)	Gallerist	Student
Caretaker	Head of public programs	Tour attendee
Collector	Infant	Tour guide
$ $ $ $ $ $ $ $ $ $ $		
Curator (celebrity)	Installation team	Visitor (accidental)
Curator (in denial)	Intern	Visitor (interested)
Curator (regular)	Modernist	
Curator (self-obsessed)	Museum director	

Having been led from the periphery to the heart of the exhibition, all the different colors merge. Indeed, you have been misled several times, when your movements activated sensors that triggered shadow plays, lighting effects, voices, and a playlist of average pop songs. The beginning and end become increasingly difficult to discern, and there may well be no such linearity at play here. In order to let the feedback loop come full circle you traveled the four routes and lost track several times: some spiraled, others joined up again at the beginning. The green line always moved at angles, making full stops, colons, and semicolons at irregular intervals through the built structures, architectural interventions, and clutter, stopping suddenly and then, if you were lucky enough to find it, continuing again. It has been a great journey so far, right?[1]

1   This entry was written with the exhibition "Alejandro Jodorowsky"—after the eponymous filmmaker—in mind, presented at the CAPC musée d'art contemporain, Bordeaux, in 2015, which made use of an exhibition architecture design by artist Andreas Angelidakis. The exhibition employed tarot as an ambiguous guiding principle and motif for navigating through the exhibition, a route that might equally be considered as a system with its own proper subject matter, working in parallel and in addition to the works presented.

→

1   Walter Benjamin, "Unpacking My Library" [1931], in *Illuminations*, trans. Harry Zorn (London: Pimlico, 1999), 61.

③

**ART
HANDLING**

We are unpacking the crates. Yes we are. The mood is not elegiac, but is rather one of anticipation, as Walter Benjamin would say.[1] However, there is actually no "we" to be found in this operation. Having climbed the rungs of institutional wellbeing, from the precarious freelance curator brigade to the contracted institutional agent, and thus having secured a more stable, or at least a more continuous sense of income, with the associated increase in leisure activities and biennial visits, I have simultaneously experienced a steady decline of onsite responsibility. Or, rather, a deskilling on the level of my physical interactions with art objects. To grip and grapple, to touch, handle, place, and position have become essayistic and reflective actions, withdrawn to the level of vocal and textual exercises, and I am becoming increasingly disconnected from my earlier physical engagement. In a sense my body has become a vessel, a mode of transportation that simply escorts my brain to its required destination—this is also partially enhanced by the scale of the institution and its consequently strict insurance policy. The coordination between eye and hand has severed over the past years, and, I suspect, a side effect of which being a poisonous cocktail of neurologically challenged dance moves, common among curators and other immaterial laborers, clearly on display on the dance floor at parties.

Withdrawing a bit further, I observe the compartmentalized nature of the organizational mesh I happen to be part of. Curious things pass before my eyes, effectively consisting of the head technician and my designated art handler creating a boundary with a piece of red-and-white-stripped danger tape—demarcating a "safe zone" around the object that now actively excludes myself and other unauthorized staff members. The rules of health, safety, and liability impinge heavily on the shoulders of those bodies unlicensed to touch, move, and engage with the works they have been entrusted to care for.

I am becoming increasingly sober, inscribing the idea of the art handler to an economic system in which over- and underinsured bodies in various material states are granted the authority to preside over one another.

⟼

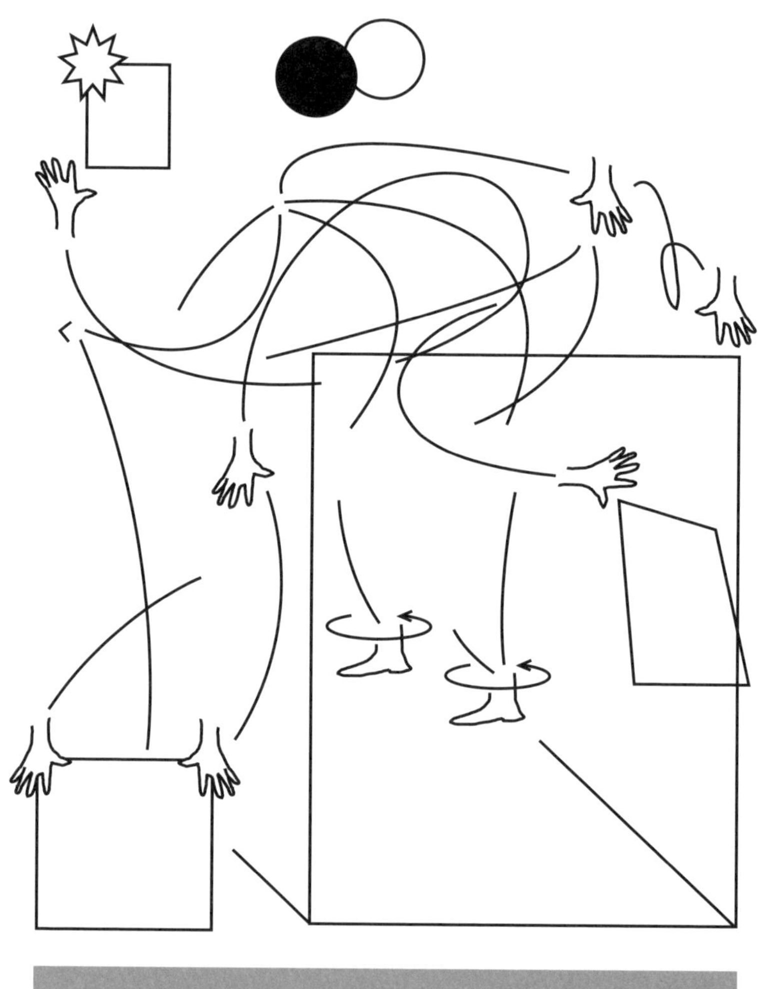

In moving away from a general notion of the public, and in making one's reading of exhibitions more specific and grounded, we could assert that the art audience is distinct from the general public. We could narrate a shift from the homogeneous phantom limb that is "out there" and "reached for" (the public), to a fragmented group of individuals that become imbedded in and applied to a specific event. Or, in other words, we could start to think of the audience as rising to the occasion.

Here we see the audience as the "acknowledgers" of what is presented; as truth-seeking onlookers who become the subjects that carry and convey those parts inherent to the situation and circumstances of the event. As both participatory narrator and eyewitness, the audience member is the figure who authenticates and acknowledges the narrative, they are induced, and equally induce themselves as pieces of evidence that renders an event's immediacy credible.

Let us speculate further and think of the audience member as a type of portable memory storage, a hard disk of sorts. As less of a human and more a set of characteristics, the audience member carries a hybridized form of documentation accumulated via the events and encounters in which they have been activated, and introduced themselves to. Their memory already patchy and full of lapses, confusing primary and secondary experiences over and over again, the audience member still comes prepared to make a narrative reading of any encounter, persistent in their attempts to construct a whole out of dislocated and unhinged fragments. These (paranoid) readings have developed from specific expectations and anticipations that are redolent of narrative form, informed and diluted by the audience member's existing knowledges and epistemological maps. In the resubmission of the event, in its recalling and retelling, the hard disk provides a supplement to a supplement, a version to a version, but one that is already an entirely different event.

⑤
AUDIO GUIDE

You are hearing voices, you are possessed.[1] For a given duration, a voice will make itself heard: a sound file played and distributed from a portable device, through a cable, toward a set of headphones.[2] A voice closely pressed to your ear, uttering coherently written passages about what is to be seen, what must remain unseen, and the factoids that can never be seen. The only opt-out options are detaching the headphones from your head, switching off the sound, uploading hacking software, or drowning the device in some kind of liquid. However, now that you are "wearing" this audio guide, the experience is already underway. You are ready. While there are many things to be said about involuntary audio guides that are handed out at exhibition entrances, accepted due to institutional pressure and group conformity, let us depart on a tour you decided on out of your own free will and perhaps even paid for.

Now that you are nestled between headphones and cut off from exterior sounds, there is no reason for you to speak. Let me tell you. Let me give you a sense of direction. That is what I am for. Am I not? Would you be surprised if I told you that we will soon be facing a major incongruity? Incongruous indeed, as I am going to speak for those things that would have said exactly the same if they (or you, for that matter) were able to speak in the same language. I am almost certain you did not take this into consideration, which is, to some extent, default of our relation, as I pacify your thoughts and give you object lessons while bypassing the object's own language and speech altogether. I will affirm most of the preselected art objects you are about to see, and leave them to hang on their translation into my text. What do you think about that? Perhaps you were not really able to think during my monologue. No questions? Good. Let us move on.

Have you been thinking about what we have just seen in the short interval of silence between what I am saying now and what I said before? No? Good. I see you have been navigating toward the next number. I know, since this is the interactive part where you get to press the number and I start to talk about what is in front of us. Now that we are talking, do you know about my hybrid successors, my hi-tech superiors? You know them? These are the audio guides with sensors that respond to the movement of your body in an exhibition space.

At this point, I feel I must excuse the nature of my conduct so far. You see, I was preprogrammed, hence the hammering and seemingly objective tone of my voice. I have not been of much help, have I? Yes, I responded to your calls, but I was hoping for some more conversation and feedback. You must understand that my vocabulary is rather limited, my syntaxes are prefabricated. I am only good for a stock monologue. I must apologize.

1   Entry best enjoyed while playing the song "The Jezebel Spirit" from the album *My Life in a Bush of Ghosts* (1981) by Brian Eno and David Byrne.

2   An initial observation on the nature of the audio guide consists of the fact that the human tour guide has been replaced by a device emitting a human voice, often in a language of your own choice. Here we could consider further possibilities of other-dimensional languages entering the frame: sound compositions, commentary provided by a cat, a guide in dialogue mode, posing dubious questions, and so on.

BENCH, CHAIR, STOOL

Can a piece of furniture act as a kind of choreographer? Does a chair utter an unwritten spatial language that we do not quite recognize? Can a chair propose a subtle interplay between movements and bodies, actively altering the composition and makeup of a given situation, and the circulation and distribution of the other actors within it? The chair is a director of movement and the body, and is simultaneously a movement and a body itself; the chair-as-choreographer enacts its own script. In this frame, we could argue that the chair is far from being a "mere" prop, a passive lump of reality deployed by others in their search for comfort. Instead, it is the chair that dictates the interactions at hand. I am not using "dictate" to suggest that the chair is an incompliant object as such—as we might observe in the work of Bruno Munari, when he attempts to seek comfort in an uncomfortable armchair—but rather to suggest that the chair's inherent characteristics and qualities must be maintained, to a certain resembling extent, in order to speak about and work alongside the formal and material connotations underpinning and informing the concept of a chair proper. That is to say, although there are endless possible variations in the *form* of the chair, or what could possibly function *as* a chair—although this would be a discussion concerned with "seating"—we cannot simply pick and choose, exhaust and undermine the fundamental concept of the chair by demanding it adhere to whatever we would like it to become. In order to subsist, the chair has to be respected as a concept and a subject in its own definitive right—and the same applies to the stool and the bench. A chair's refusal to be reduced to a slab of material reality is evidenced on the level of the agency exercised by the chair and its potential for spontaneous, unpredictable change over time; it is able to endure shifts in its composition and makeup, and even when broken, a chair is still recognizable as such. The chair is a robust figure that presides over its own being, conduct, and speech through resisting, steering, and shaping interaction, while simultaneously playing a part in the formation of new relations.

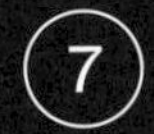

BLACK BOX

This is my third visit. For three consecutive weeks I have made an appointment with thought. An appointment with myself and the objective of uninterrupted and solitary thinking. Since the feedback loop between myself and my curious habits has not come full circle yet, I decided to enter a process of rendering myself sensitive by retreating into a thinking cabin.[1]

I have found a more than adequate spot, a place of solitary confinement that suits my contemplative endeavor. I tried a variety of spaces before coming here, including my own apartment, although the general household clutter and the semiotics of the kitchen proved too misleading.[2]

My temporary thinking cabin is located in an exhibition that focuses on the immaterial material of sound as an overlooked category within art history. To get to the exhibition, and my thinking cabin, first, I am sitting on a busy bus, then I am sitting in a room. From the white cube I make my way through the gray hangar and into the black box, but no break in my muddy, gray-matter thought seems to occur.[3]

A soundtrack is playing, somewhat of an elusive siren song, which does not disturb me in the slightest. I am applying myself to thinking, but now I see that the space is insulated with Styrofoam silencers, which I had failed to notice on my first two visits.

In this mental vacuum things only appear gradually; like invisible ink, the space is charged with subtle connections that will settle and present themselves to me of their own accord, it is merely a matter of time. As I slouch on the bench seat, I focus on my retreat into this neural vat and distribute my thinking more evenly.

I hear people approaching my thinking cabin. Just before they enter, I quickly adjust my compromised posture and try to act natural. What is the appropriate way to act naturally in the darkness? One of the visitors starts

$\longmapsto$

whistling along to the siren song. I lost it, again. The seemingly unobtainable object of thought. He is probably feeling somewhat uneasy in the process of retinal acclimatization to the space and whistling to announce his presence to the alien body (me) that had installed itself prior to his arrival. In any case, the creation of the hermetic seal, deemed so necessary to establish an equilibrium of thought, or at least to prompt unsuccessful attempts to do so, has been effectively distorted.

I shall have to book another appointment with thought, I think, and think we must.

1   This entry departs from a scenario described by Enrique Vila-Matas in *The Illogic of Kassel*, in which the writer-protagonist aims to make an appointment with thought by creating a thinking cabin in Kassel, and by frequenting a pitch-black room (hosting a performance work by Tino Sehgal) to come to terms with prior occurrences in his life, effectively distorted by the performing bodies that keep him from thinking and challenge his last grip on sanity. Enrique Vila-Matas, *The Illogic of Kassel* (New York: New Directions, 2015).

2   Reference to Martha Rosler's video work entitled *Semiotics of the Kitchen* (1975).

3   The "gray hangar" is an interesting addition to the common and oppositional exhibition settings of the white cube and the black box, and often takes the shape of squats, industrial lofts, or abandoned spaces that retain their initial (non-art) architectural connotations. From an interview with artist Michael Portnoy: Hendrik Folkerts, "Two Musicals (Part I): Michael Portnoy: Relational Stalinism: The Musical," *Metropolis M* (June 10, 2016), http://metropolism.com/features/two-musicals-part-i-michael-port.

BOOK BEHIND GLASS

A closed book behind glass. The presentation of a thing in such a straightforward way that it seemingly needs no explanation. By letting the closed volume evoke and establish parallel references, it has the ability to hold many points of view in suspension—for their part, the visitor screens the materiality of the surface and the notes on the cover. In the grammar of display, a book behind glass provokes a conflicting series of concepts, of both a transparent and an opaque nature. Here, glass functions in a way that, instead of allowing one to probe for an essence on the level of the obscured contents, only enables one to scan the surface. The given fact that glass is transparent is irrelevant; rather, the sheet of glass is a mediating thing that stands in between a number of different actors: the visitor and the undisclosed book. To be glass is to encourage, even instigate, an oppositional split between parties, to withhold certain knowledges and keep the formation of an informed position at bay. A seemingly neutral agent (perhaps not dissimilar to a Swiss guard) that, while wary that their presence is both suppressive and misleading, and silently retreating accordingly, prevents you from passing, with or without permission, nevertheless. Performing in front of the book, at all times.

The thing performing: a book lodged between a wall and a sheet of glass, held there by four screws; a book placed in a vitrine, behind glass; a book on a shelf, covered by a glass case. In short, glass as the middle ground between presenting and securing provides ample possibilities, also available in Perspex. We pass the banality of potential health and safety violations. The health and safety of the book, as artifact, as reference, as irreplaceable instance of cultural heritage, as overinsured body of knowledge, is secured and present, but remains inaccessible.

Presenting a book behind glass, depending on the context, veers somewhere between pretense and pretentiousness: on the one hand, there is an implicit pointing from within the exhibition toward a suggested set of references elsewhere, outside, and planting "work to be done" on the lap of the curious reader of surfaces. On the other hand, a body of knowledge

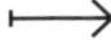

is present but feigned—at the level of the exhibition—and cannot be disclosed for fear of damaging the book as object. This book is an undisclosed object of knowledge, literally lodged behind a sheet of glass, as no question regarding its contents can be answered by saying that there is a mind knowing it (unless the visitor has managed to read the contents of the book beforehand). Here, the book is foregrounded as an object of reference, while simultaneously implying a distance between the object of knowledge it has come stand in for and the text that has been omitted from the view of the visitor. Freed from the burden of having to involve interaction and, in some cases, the duties of communicating altogether, the relation between visitor and book is preempted, numbed to the extent of being perceived as a sign pointing to a dead end. There might as well be a label next to the book describing the contents of the object—an additional level of institutional opacity—or some pieces of information on the jacket might become legible during the visitor's viewing process, their meaning then solidified in relation to other works in the exhibition.

To be a book behind glass is to serve first and foremost as an indication of not yet knowing; it might trigger a referential curiosity toward the things in the world that come into being in the moment of encounter, things that remain in the background, and demand that a leap be taken in order to figure out the pieces of information they withhold.

A book behind glass. Dictated but not read.

OPEN CALL FOR EXHIBITION PROPOSALS

The Embassy of Switzerland in South Korea, which relocated last year from Seoul to the island of Ulleungdo, is proud to announce the fourth edition of its Open Call for Exhibition Proposals. In an ongoing collaboration with The Swiss Arts Council Pro Helvetia, the embassy is looking for thought-provoking proposals that expand and push past the conventional definitions and dimensions of the exhibition medium. Revolving around a yearly central theme, set out and juried by the Swiss cultural attaché based on Ulleungdo, in close consultation with a team of local scouts, this year's call will focus on proposals highlighting the thematic potential of "an exhibition that carries its brain outside of its body."

Conceived and commissioned within the daily reality of the Chtulucene,[1] its confrontational conditions and unforeseen impacts on the lives of the inhabitants of Ulleungdo, and elsewhere, the call necessitates proposals that incorporate an ongoing engagement and dialogue with the community and situation at hand. Applicants should be wary that the newly opened cultural center, as an integral activity of The Embassy of Switzerland and its aim to promote Swiss culture and foster dialogue among different audiences, has been repurposed to accommodate the substantial influx of the public seeking refuge from the irregular occurrence of high tides and severe heat waves, and will thus not host the outcome of this year's call. However, in remaining concerned with and dedicated to its audiences, the center aims to continue its activities throughout the year by making available its exhibition spaces not only for shelter, but equally by implementing a lively program of forums, events, talks, and discussions around thinking and living with each other, as well as teaching classes on deimatic behavior and display.

In response to the call, successful proposals will show a keen interest in the fabric of daily life, further advanced by inventive solutions for transposing artistic interventions onto the remainder of available public spaces

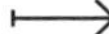

on Ulleungdo, among, by way of example, billboards, elevated patches of land, online environments, and other performative and outward movements of reaching beyond conventional contexts for the exhibiting of art. Furthermore, proposals should establish firm connections between the cultural center and its active community, and, by extension, be receptive to and affective toward the large variety of honorary vertebrates, among them squids and octopuses, that populate the island. As our kinfolk before and with us, the call supports proposals capable of implementing metamorphic zones that are inclusive toward the call and response from and to the various life forms inhabiting the island; moving from an exhibition vacuum toward the material formalization of the possible in a life continuum.

The call has an application-based process, and is open to all who deem the call to be of interest. There is no condition of residency or citizenship.

1 "So, I think a big new name, actually more than one name, is warranted. Thus, Anthropocene, Plantationocene, and Capitalocene (Andreas Malm's and Jason Moore's term before it was mine). I also insist that we need a name for the dynamic ongoing sym-chthonic forces and powers of which people are a part, within which ongoingness is at stake. Maybe, but only maybe, and only with intense commitment and collaborative work and play with other terrans, flourishing for rich multispecies assemblages that include people will be possible. I am calling all this the Chthulucene —past, present, and to come. [...] 'My' Chthulucene, even burdened with its problematic Greek-ish tendrils, entangles myriad temporalities and spatialities and myriad intra-active entities-in-assemblages—including the more-than-human, other-than-human, inhuman, and human-as-humus." Donna Haraway, "Anthropocene, Capitalocene, Plantationocene, Chthulucene: Making Kin," *Environmental Humanities* 6 (2015): 160.

Proposals should include the following documents:

• A concept outlining the framework, as well as the aims
  and ambitions of the exhibition project
• A portfolio of proposed artists and participants,
  with accompanying visual material
• A recent CV
• A preliminary budget

Closing date for applications is: June 14, 2088, 17:00 GMT+9

Proposals can be submitted by sending an e-mail to:
chthulucene@protonmail.ch

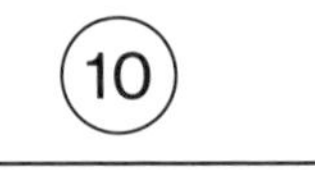

Remarks on the history of cable concealing.

General knowledge from an often cited but as yet unwritten household manual draws a sketchy and turbulent picture of the treatment of cables within the domestic environment. As a commonly understood rule set, the act of hiding cables is perfected by some to such an extent that it comes to indicate the mastery of some kind of sport not yet accounted for. Not necessarily or exclusively undertaken as a measure for mere safety within the household (slapstick tripping), hiding cables can represent the urge for an aesthetic wellbeing for those that prefer a neat smoothness over letting the matter drift as the cable itself is wont to do. Here we can see the deployment of apparatuses, a multitude of fixtures, that make cables conform to the straight lines of walls, or follow the angles of room corners. Additionally, tricks are put in place to further cloak and disguise cables throughout living rooms, among them the usage of modified baseboards and storage cabinets with holes in their backs.

Similar tricks find their inscription in the space of the exhibition, and perhaps even under similar guiding principles of obscuring rather than revealing, and of not allowing for any visible interaction between cables and their neighbors. We may envisage a technician, with the eyes of a cold silent killer—in a manner of automatic, learned, or perhaps instructed behavior—grappling with various material situations in need of maneuvering. Here we find groves, ridges, and encasings specifically devised for the routing of cables; tape and cable clips in different camouflage shades that mimic the color of the walls or floors. What is to be said about the additional effort and labor that is put into the act of hiding cables, when the decision to do so is almost always undisputed and automatically processed? There is arguably a stable and recognizable pattern of automation, one that must reach beyond a homogenous bunch of technicians with an equal preference for neatness. Perhaps the persistent and firm beliefs inherited from modernist ancestry dictate how cables are treated: the space for potential thought and mental participation that is deliberately left open between viewer and artwork should not be occupied by nuisances, but instead should be a liminal, clean slate that allows for the formation of mental

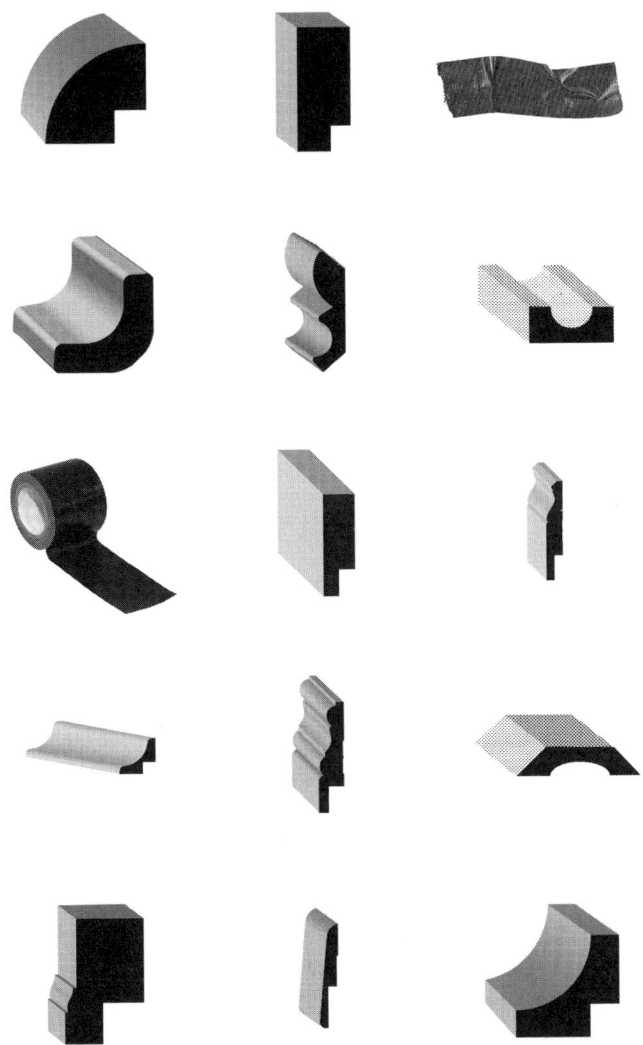

⟼

building blocks, mostly generated by the viewer. The additional effort to get rid of the "clutter" may come to stand for the feigned autonomy of both the work and the viewer, as the visibility of a network of cables could reveal the various levels of dependency between actors. It is not the architectural and structural "thickening" of the exhibition space, via the visibility of its operating systems, supporting inhabitants, and infrastructures, but the maintaining of a deliberate illusion of autonomy that fails to account for the non-human and non-artwork elements which support our existence and the coming-into-being of an exhibition as a dynamic and fragmented whole. Indeed, supportive material objects can be difficult to recognize because they often reside beyond our experience of time and space within an exhibition. Observing and acknowledging the deep, elusive reality of these seemingly withdrawn objects would allow us to recognize the material world that underlies and enables our everyday lives. To show the act of showing would be to lay bare linkages and enablers in the exhibition: to anticipate a breakthrough in the space of potential thought instigated between viewer and artwork, as a consciousness-raising act for readily existing mutual dependencies. No more "clean" viewing, no more hiding.

CEILING

Walls and floors, sometimes corners, with or without domestic attributes and ornamentation, have most often taken center stage as both subjects and fertilizing hosts within the exhibition space. In terms of the ceiling, it could be compared to a bass player in a band, the person who simultaneously lurks in the shadows and is crucial to the formation of a fundamental grounding for the other band members, giving depth and density, rhythm and pace to the otherwise shallow utterance of vocal chords and modulations. Although, to think of a ceiling providing grounding for an exhibition space does seem like a contradiction in terms. At the same time the ceiling would surely be noticed—at last—when gone missing, but let us consider it in terms of its obscured given-ness, rather than further cultivating a kind of horticultural thinking that would revolve around scenarios of exhibition spaces without ceilings being subjected to the heroic weather conditions of the universe. In this sense curators often speak of "a thickening of the walls" when wall-based spatial features are made apparent and enhanced through the installation elements of an exhibition, and move from being the withdrawn, architectural foundations of the space into the foreground as active elements of the exhibition text. In the case of the ceiling, however, its performance and action in the space and time of an exhibition is less evident. Often adorned with skylights, LED strips, air conditioning units, and fluorescent fixtures, the ceiling seems to carry certain disadvantages compared to the other prominently featured surfaces that are kept clean and ready to perform.

Essentially and structurally undervalued, and thus often subjugated according to the logic of conventional display politics (bottom-up instead of top-down), we find the ceiling pierced with the holes, plugs, hooks, and screws of previously suspended screens, projectors, and hanging art objects. There is a logic to be changed: the ceiling can and should be prioritized for its role in serving other parasites, rather than being constantly overlooked in its current functionality. Let us make a plea for a more transporting and generative principle beyond the reductive compartmentalizations of ceiling, floor, and wall, toward a more contained and embodied sense of wallness, suspended between volumes and subject to the less optimization-focused viewing conditions dictated by the conventional regimes of vision inducement.

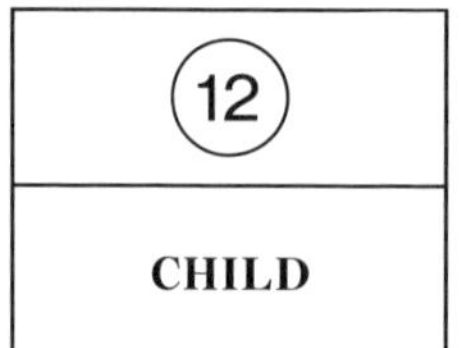

*"Darf ich mein Lichtschwert mit
in die Ausstellung nehmen?"*

*"Nein. Aus Rücksicht auf die anderen Besucher
sind alle Waffen-Repliken oder andere Requisiten
innerhalb der Ausstellung nicht gestattet."*[1]

The child is commonly lodged somewhere between a wall and a monitor. Here they are to be found, reaching to disconnect the power cables, only to quickly find out that the connectors do not correspond with the battery plug of their more up-to-date model of retina novelty. There is a tendency of the child to hide in enclosed spaces where cables or Pokémon reside, often with unforeseen and disastrous consequences for the stable continuation of an exhibition—a risk which has led to the installing of unsuccessful technologies such as keypad locks on electronic exhibition devices to avoid interrupted video screenings. Furthermore, they tend to remain in these shady exhibition nooks until their device runs out of battery, at which point they disconnect, emerge, and busy themselves with the further eradication and demolition of art objects.

As a seemingly approachable and empathetic subject on first encounter, the child is often hard to differentiate from and often mistaken for the larger versions of personhood. As snappy dressers with opinions that astutely confront the adult specimen's tendency to overlook certain readings within the exhibition, combined with infinitely deep-pocketed, influential peer-to-peer networks, the child must not be provoked as a consequence of an adult's tantrum. The result would be counterproductive: activating an instantaneous "mob" of child peers, negatively grading the respective institution on online platforms—while confusing the fact that the institution is not its parent's property.

Furthermore, to station a child in an education department, be it temporarily or for more prolonged periods, may dislodge their feeling of belonging to a world of instant connectivity and constant motion. Against persistent and popular beliefs, the cultural benefits of art education for the child do not necessarily foster a healthy appetite for future conversations with

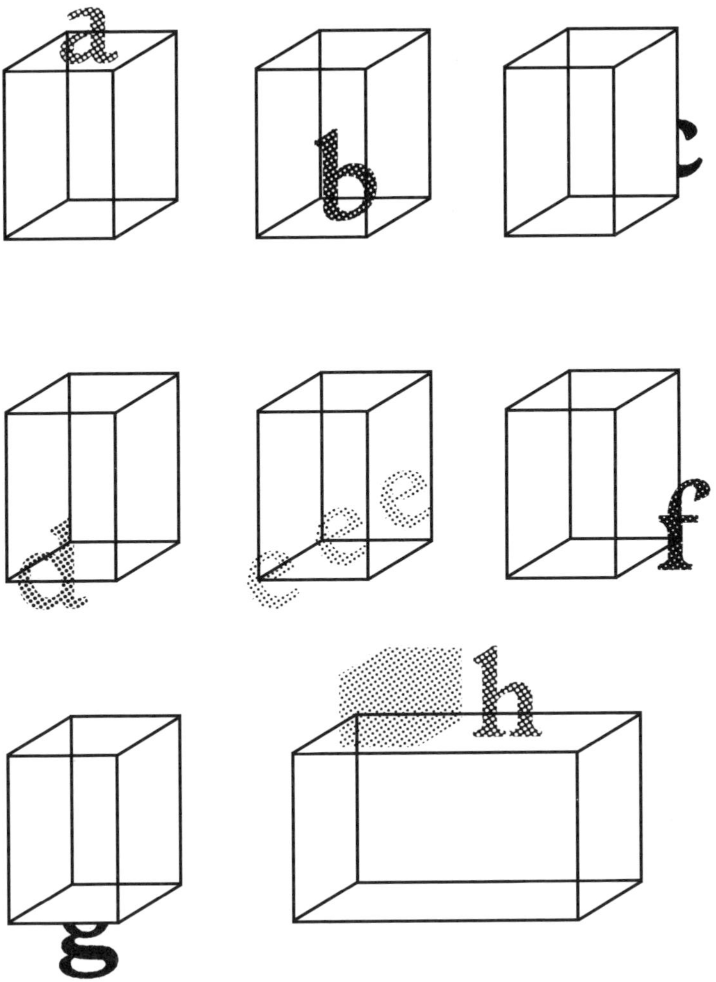

Compositions with child and plinth

other educated guests. Rather, the child is employed as the leading figure within specialized institutional attempts to increase the margin of funding for the actual exhibition program, and is thus more of an agent in the advanced-capitalist scheme of absorbing funding grants obtained through the implementation of surrogate and imaginary child-sized exhibitions, which are much more cost-effective.

Eventually, an adult specimen might decide to subject the child to an encounter with an artwork proper, in which case the child is to be watched at all times. In so doing, the adult is advised to wrap a child in jargon, or to place the child on an empty plinth with a light snack, for the sake of brevity. To make the child understand the core concepts of the exhibition through a verbal tirade is a conditioning principle to be avoided, unless solely consisting of jargon. Ultimately, the child will collapse, exhausted from the experience, and lapse into an extended period of hibernation.

1   "'Can I bring my lightsaber to the exhibition?' 'No. Out of consideration for other visitors, all replica weapons and other props are also forbidden inside the exhibition.'" From the frequently asked questions section found on the website of the "Star Wars Identities – The Exhibition" in Munich. "HÄUFIG GESTELLTE FRAGEN," Star Wars Identities–The Exhibition website, accessed July 13, 2016, http://de.starwarsidentites.com/#!/faq/details.

CLAPPING

Commonly employed to release and expel the spirits that inhabit a given space after a performance, clapping, or the more collective round of applause, could be considered as both a social and spatial event—even as an event in itself.

Within the context of an exhibition, a performance would normally be concluded by a round of applause, the crowd's closing remark, their seal of approval. "Normally," insofar as we could posit applause as a normative ethic and logic that completes a performance; not so much as a collective affirmation of appreciation or a sign of understanding aesthetic value, but rather as a built-in mechanism, a means to an end, adopted through stable patterns of repetition. A cardinal example of such learned behavior is manifested in the exhibition, where it is rather uncommon to clap before a performance, when participants appear for the first time, as a timely round of clapping must be based on past achievements. In the exhibition, performance participants are not applauded for being themselves *per se*, as there is a common understanding of the performer as serving the work, rather than the propagation of a specific persona.

Furthermore, clapping seems to signify a primordial value attribute that lets humans represent themselves through an action—clapping as the moment when a group of people become a public—that is increasingly more often rhythmical rather than random—although exceptions of polyphonic clapping remain. As a type of mass, nonverbal communication, a collective act of clapping puts forward and underscores a dynamic situation in which the point of attention expands from the performance out into the entire space. Clapping posits a sub-architecture in which the clappers take into account the given spatial distances and parameters of their surroundings, as well as the social nature of the event. One person clapping, two persons clapping, eighteen persons clapping—the single perspective dissolves, blocked blood circulation flows again, the reverberation time of a room is measured, and as the clapping dies down the public folds and retreats.

**COAT OF
PAINT**

A white, freshly painted wall is an eloquent topic to cover. On first impression, it is a robust conversation partner that would give substance to a text almost immediately, without the need for excessive framing, tweaking, or having to mask over something absent. A subject of interrogation that is simultaneously its own object, or an object that is simultaneously its own subject. A rights-bearing subject-object that posits its own textual framework and becomes the breathing archive of various institutional imprints—a stratification accumulated by the wall over time, single-handedly, while remaining taciturn about its biographical underpinnings.

Not only is there a silence implied when facing a freshly coated wall, it also has a mystical reticence, since there is no conversation to speak of. Not yet at least. And so we find ourselves hovering in front of a silent mass that is both yet to speak and a projective surface.

You cannot simply pick and choose a material volume to speak to, let alone poke the wall with a stick to see what is has to say, or what it has sneakily obscured or hidden behind its surface. One might agree that the fresh coat of paint should be approached differently, through poetics perhaps, slowly working at it from the inside, so that in our aim of describing the performance of coating as truthfully as possible, we may observe that it alters states and that the newly applied coat has sunk shyly into its own background.

Then, what is to be gathered from the exterior of the wall with its fresh coat, now it has become seemingly stable and impossible to think of as separate or distinct from the wall surface, and is more or less settling itself as a collateral element of the surrounding architecture? Or, what information can we explicate from the residual contours of the recently applied paint, as observed on the surface, which is slowly drying inward toward no discernable core? You might change your mind about a coat of paint being just another cosmetic premise, a high-speed opacity application, a clean surface for another exhibition. Let us quickly cover up the traces, the scuff marks, the small holes, all the sign language, the graphite marks and measures… Nobody will notice. No dirty hands, please.

This cover-up strikes us as an evasive maneuver that by no means takes account of or responsibility for all that was internalized through the application of numerous paint layers: the minor histories, the ghosts of previous states, and the hordes of bacteria that have organically settled themselves between the layers.

You make a plea for a genealogy of the minor histories of painted coats, one with both an opaqueness that is similar to their now-obscured legacy and a potential to register, catalog, and store.

Slowly swallowed by its pride and ambition, with the mounting of exhibition after exhibition, the space gradually becomes smaller and smaller, coat after coat. How does it feel to work from within, surrounded by freshly white painted coats of

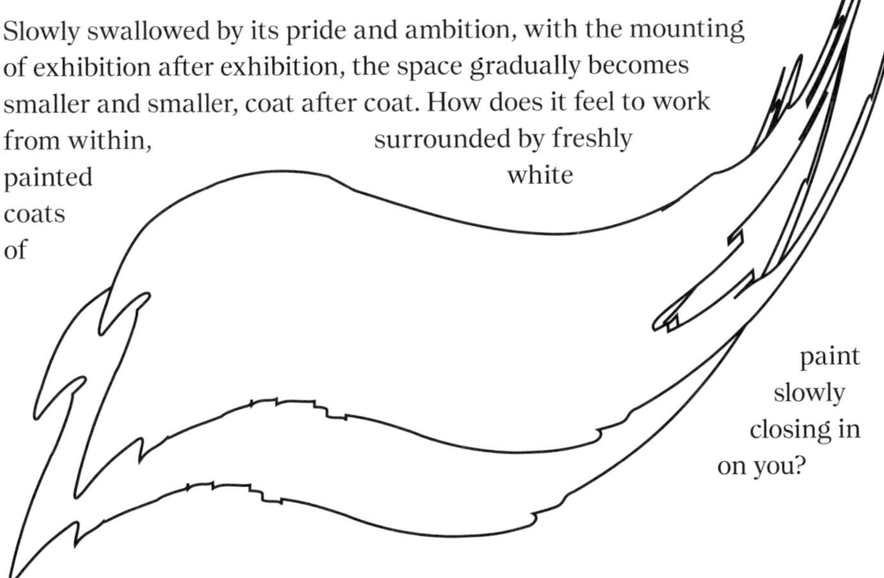

paint slowly closing in on you?

(15)

COLUMN

On their way out of the exhibition space, the phenomenologist suffered a heart attack. Together with their penultimate heartbeat—as any attempt of a final leap of the heart was as yet indeterminate, at least considering the good hope encrusted on their chest and by means of their spasms—that punctuated their collapse on the sidewalk, and by a general ceasing of the blood flow and oxygen delivery to their brain, the same building they had just visited came down, transformed by an implosion of its weighty architecture into a gray cloud of dust particles and debris. Although it was uncertain to what extent the phenomenologist had ceased to exist or had even been buried in the debris, an observer of the scene was finally able to locate the body and drag it aside.

As the reanimation procedures were executed in the right order, it seemed that certain memory fragments were recalled by the phenomenologist, who, just before their anticipated submission to the society of angels, started to mumble the opening phrase of Joy Division's song "Atmosphere": "Walk in silence... Don't walk away..." The reason for the distress was not related to the phenomenologist's intermittent heartbeat, nor a confusion between primary and secondary retention for that matter, but, rather, it concerned the imagined collapse of Bergsonian, cone-like volumes that resembled columns. In fact, the phenomenologist had collapsed and passed out, although only temporarily. However, having the four columns in their mind, the ones that were arranged in a square and around three meters apart, and positioned in the middle of the exhibition space to support the rooftop windows, that the phenomenologist had so consciously experienced as frustrating when moving through the exhibition space, well, each of them remained standing, and so did the surrounding building. Paradoxical, indeed, but less so when we consider the obstinate mindset of the phenomenologist, who relied all too heavily on the idealist viewpoint of matter's dependency on the mind. With his seizure, the consciously apprehended columns also ceased to exist, which in turn provoked the theoretical collapse of the building.

The four columns remained withdrawn from the conscious perception of the majority of the exhibition visitors by means of a readily asserted given-ness: the subconscious cognition of forms that go unseen because they have turned into stable, recognizable patterns—a perceptual glut.

The phenomenologist begged to differ, as the presence of that which sounded like a slide projector was largely obscured by a column that stood in the foreground and presented itself to them as a block limiting their field of vision. In stubbornly circumnavigating the column without moving themselves at all, the phenomenologist got some of their mental technicians—who were invisible—to reduce the weight of the air enough so they could lower the height of the column. This lead to a number of sightlines and images of the underlying situation, and they were quite delighted.

With this movement of thought, the columns became all the more prominent as the anticipated slide projector turned out to be a piece of black marble on a stand, and the rhythmical, somewhat militant clicking sounds remained present, but were located elsewhere. Additionally, the columns were not only required to support the roof, as architectural devices, but were equally thought of in terms of their exhibition potential, of marking the outer ends of the temporary walls placed between them. Accidentally, the phenomenologist was not able to overcome their unsuccessful thought experiment and could only remain fixated on how the white, thick, plastered columns withheld an envisioned slide projector that was not there.

To the phenomenologist's great frustration, the columns remained. What is left of a consciously experienced object that has been abandoned by the disappearing of another perceiving subject who claimed and celebrated the dependency of matter on the mind?

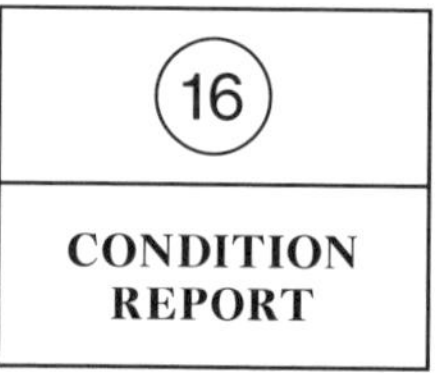

CONDITION REPORT

Three consecutive weeks after the opening—the exhibition being halfway through its run—the team is provided with a unique moment to reflect on the condition of the exhibition. Also, some visitors are growing increasingly suspicious of its general state.

EXHIBIT A

The team nervously makes a close reading of the exhibition, observing the traces and byproducts it has accumulated. With a forensic eye, the net worth of endogenous substances is established and analyzed. Exploring the evidential facts in particular, human traces appear to be quite substantial in number, although spores, seeds (predominantly dandelion seedlings), and dog hair were also unearthed. The exhibition space was found to be covered with stains and (mostly unintentional) scuff marks, footprints (in different sizes and patterns and carrying various gradations of soil and other, more chemical materials), as well as hand- and fingerprints (with acidity and fat levels of varying degrees).

*

EXHIBIT B

The team's second, more in-depth review of the different spaces disclosed further bodily matter. In one space, they were able to reconstruct a previous event that included a performative element in which a crowd most likely felt pressured to move from the center toward the outer edges of the room. This movement was partially confirmed by the manifestation of peripheral trace elements, namely factions of hair congregating around the entire boarder of the room. This was noted by the team as unusual, insofar as human hair and dust particles normally share a tendency to nestle together in corners where gusts of wind transport them, and leave them there to settle otherwise unaffected.

*

EXHIBIT C

As observed from floor perspective: the lower half of a full-length vitrine is covered with handprints and saliva, but from 60 centimeters upward the object remains relatively untouched.

*

EXHIBIT D

Other displays showing signs of bodily interference were to be found; everything from passive and collateral behaviors to the traces of more direct attempts at access, engagement, and interaction. The team found shelves with skin tissue and tallow on the edges, sections of plinths with different pH levels on their top surfaces, which will eventually manifest as yellow-green hues, and upholstered seats and benches showing signs of wear, most visible at the points where the fabric was frequently distressed.

*

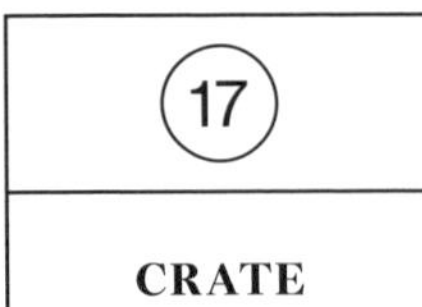

A short commentary on the crate.

From the forest, to the workbench, into storage, and onto the fire.

In order to become one, you must be many. Luckily you find yourself to be among peers. You are a legion. A purposeful legion grown to gratify various ends. You have become a single, individual pine tree among many, in a renewable Swedish forest. Rooted in sustainable forest management, and conceived in the wake of carbon chauvinism, you will soon be supplanted by civilization.[1] That is to say, by three dedicated woodcutters and their supervisor—who never met their CEO but would like to nevertheless—in the log cabin over there. Each of these workers, in turn, play their part in another scheme of things, and in the case of the CEO this would concern managing vectors of information—our third nature—among logistics, stock exchange analysis, controlling the risks, convincing the board members, and, above all, remaining the market leader they always wished to be.

You have been relocated to the Bauhaus AG. Indeed, the retail hardware chain that always appeals to the imagination of the art historian. You have become many now. Many separate pieces, commonly named "planks." Whether you still resemble or perhaps even are a tree remains uncertain (here we might begin to recall Theseus' paradox). However, your shape-changing capacities make a weak thought experiment: from the initial tree-being in the Swedish forest to the wood-state in the Bauhaus AG, your raw and unstable matter had to be made inert so as to classify you as a workable material that could be capitalized upon. With a faint hint of that liveliness you once possessed, now so desirable, so malleable, you pass into the workshop...

Joined by other tree neighbors cleverly reengineered into sheets of plywood, you start to resemble the robust and solid form of another construct. To add to this curious amalgam, the art-handling specialist makes you foam at the mouth, and then on the inside. You, the initial whole-tree-being,

$\longmapsto$

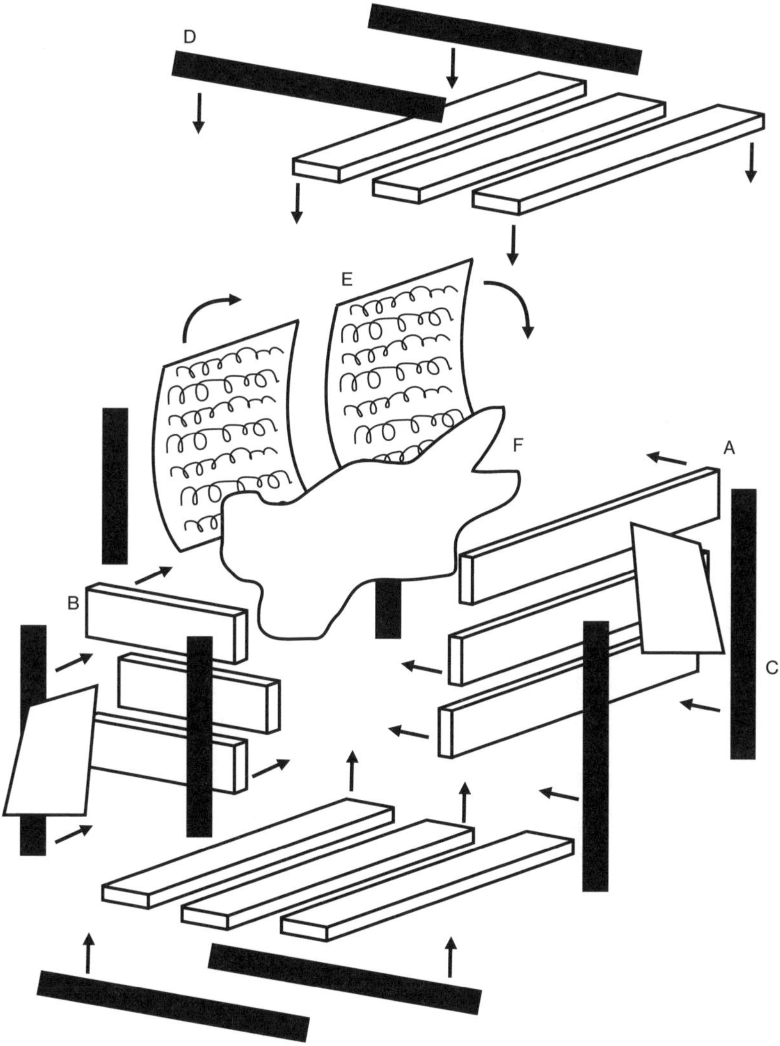

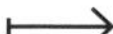

have been abandoned in light of something else: a crate. In a repetitive montage fashion, padding is finished, handles placed. We come to grips with the object of interrogation.

How to travel if you are a fetishized commodity? Through an economy of crates, a system of overly insured material bodies, in a climate where your transport makes up 35 percent of the budget. The story of your coming into being as an acting partner, as a crucial link in the chain of trafficked volumes, is mostly the story of an antihero. A story of forklifts, a life of generic rental boxes, your contents marked by a series of gallery labels stapled on your back. (This way up!) Occasionally you are put on display, as a *laissez-faire* support, a somewhat alien escort in the exhibition space, or the evidence of provenance for the thing you accompanied. You are, however, foremost a reminder of an Earth supplanted by civilization, a feedback signal for the hurtling world of things traveling.

1   "The term [carbon chauvinism] was used as early as 1973, when scientist Carl Sagan described it and other human chauvinisms that limit imagination of possible extraterrestrial life. It suggests that human beings, as carbon-based life forms who have never encountered any life that has evolved outside the Earth's environment, may find it difficult to envision radically different biochemistries." "Carbon Chauvinism," *Wikipedia*, accessed July 13, 2016, https://en.wikipedia.org/wiki/Carbon _chauvinism.

CURATOR

A curator is an unstable and shifting cluster of behavioral and performative patterns, roles, and skill sets defined according to the calls from and responses to the "different other" and the unknown, the situation at hand, its text, and the modifiable given-ness of context.

A combination of cards played accordingly, the curator as: bartender,[1] janitor, concierge, convener, instigator of social change, inventor of cognitive perception, artist, producer, author, iconoclast, censor, culture broker, infrastructural activist, research worker, employer, dealer, dynamo, tourist, catalyst, mediator for contemporary art, architect, canary or crony, poet, collaborator, arts administrator, middleperson, team leader, social engine, de facto acoustician, scholar and public spokesperson, cardboard supplier, support structure, scavenger,[2] translator, film editor, champion, controller of the visitor and purveyor of knowledge, head of […], caretaker of objects, networker, key figure of the art world, translator of theory into practice, curator.

1 *The Curator as Barman* (London: Automatic Books, 2015).

2 "Curators are scavengers. We do not make, we move. We do not produce, we frame. We are the unseen orchestrators of display. Our endeavour is subtractive. We edit. We mix. We Montage. We rework. We unwork. We feast on the pre-existing, travelling around the world in packs. Our craft is everywhere, and yet we have no product. No one is meant to see us. Feed us. But here we are. Or not. We beg you. Without others, we are nothing. And yet without us, what is there for you to see?" Quoted from a found postcard.

(19)

CURTAIN

Shifting from the back to the front, in making its move toward the main stage, the curtain starts to be a performer in its own right. Although the curtain still maintains its theatrical underpinnings in an exhibition setting, in this change to a performer position, we can observe the negotiating of different agendas corresponding to the curtain's characteristics and qualities. In its theatrical employment, the curtain poses quite clear distinctions regarding the division between front and back, and the proper places for objects. Without much ado, the theatrical curtain erects itself as a division line, as a marker of territories with different functions and behaviors; without necessitating any prior consultation about inclusion and exclusion mechanisms, the curtain is imposed and imposes itself. Frankly, the curtain has quite a key role in keeping categories discrete and tidy, in dividing objects between ready and present, visible and invisible, prop and performer, active and passive.

In its exhibition habitat, the curtain undergoes a transformation through which the demands of the center stage now apply. Here, the dividing properties of the curtain are less related to the practicalities of what is publicly foregrounded and what remains inaccessible—even when bodies start to navigate within the exhibition space—but rather come to propose a renegotiated spatial logic of diffused sight lines and perspectives that informs the exhibition space as a fragmented whole. The curtain now figures in another form of spatial writing that is both transparent and opaque in nature: it only gradually discloses the constituent objects based on the movement of the various motile performers present.

DAYLIGHT

I invite you to the staging of an exhibition in broad daylight. It makes sense. It truly does. Last time we talked in the exhibition over some casual drinks, and, in fact, it was exactly the same exhibition we are currently facing, it was at night, when nobody was looking. It was a convivial outing, for sure. All the people, their drinks, and their speeches were there. It was everything I expected, and less. In the daylight, however, those nighttime bodies have returned to being carriers of agendas, aims, and ambitions—translating their desires into different modes of action. And, clearly, nobody is here now.

It is an interesting shift, these seemingly altered states of visiting the exhibition during the day and visiting it at night. Not that we are left with much of a choice—the institutional operating bodies have allocated the daytime as the natural timeframe of the exhibition. There is conceptual transparency to be found in daylight. In the projection of daylight into the exhibition, colors appear slightly differently, the video seems painstakingly faint, there is play of geometric shadow figures appearing and disappearing in different configurations over the course of the day, and the temperature of the space changes, reaching its climax around half past two. Although there might be attempts at refusing these imposing effects, daylight always seems to find its ways through blocked windows, cracks, and gaps. Daylight is the exhibition outlaw of perceptual distortion and deterioration, as it provokes disputes over the nature of things, pressing us to negotiate how the objects displayed present themselves, and are represented differently through the added value of daylight impinging on their surfaces.

**DEHUMIDI-
FIER**

The porous boundaries between things previously thought separate are completely overrun by an error in the hygrothermograph's settings.

This particular object, commonly placed at the most discreet locations within exhibition and storage spaces, was entirely forgotten, and although it partially resurfaced through a sudden influx of spore patterns on the walls, matters severely deteriorated and it was never to be found again.

Was it the sudden dry gusts of wind, enhanced by the leak in the boiler room, that caused the relative humidity to go from a desirable 48 percent to over 70 percent overnight? Cloaked in a thick, nebulous mist, most of the exhibition spaces were entirely obscured. "Relative humidity is expressed as a percentage of moisture content in the air at a given time and temperature, and at this given time and temperature, things have gotten out of hand," climate control remarked.

The hygroscopic family, on the contrary, felt entirely "at ease" with the situation. Commonly described as the group of materials most sensitive to moisture, the hygroscopic kinfolk should have been affected the most by this radical shift, manifested through a significant increase in the level of stress within their objecthood. And, indeed, their stress materialized in a number of apparent changes, among them dimensional and chemical reactions such as warping, the dislocation of joints, splitting, the breaking of fibers, delaminating and loss of surfaces, cracking, the corrosion of metal parts, fading of dyes, crizzling of glass, crystallization and movement of salts, the disintegration and yellowing of paper, and so on, and so forth. However, met with a sense of biodeterioration, and overgrown by a velvety layer of green mold that then gave rise to a fungus with stems waving in the air, the hygroscopic kin seemed to flourish—against all odds.[1] Indeed, thriving and rapidly expanding, proliferating in the damp exhibition space, their stable and continuous growth seemed to be far from under threat.

As the hygroscopic family's wellbeing was greatly enhanced in this thermodynamic equilibrium, a legion of buzzing dehumidifying agents was sent in. The dehumidifiers, now lodged between the remnants of steadily decaying pedestals commenced sucking the liquid from the air, functioning as a pacifying agents and mediating between the various parts that had grown indistinct, their lungs filling up with the porous boundaries between things.

1   This entry was partially inspired by: Anna Lowenhaupt Tsing, *The Mushroom at the End of the World: On the Possibility of Life in Capitalist Ruins* (Princeton and Oxford: Princeton University Press, 2015).

DEPOT

There is a hole in the exterior wall of the institution, a hole through which all the objects bound for display enter. A hole that is equally large enough to let wildlife in. Closed off by a roller door, the hole is directly followed by a room: a mouth and a tongue through which objects enter, are provided with a soft landing, and gradually digest into art objects. This intermediate space, often called a depot, or a holding room, is fitted with the capacity to show the thing-ness of whatever is yet to be unpacked. Crates, tubes, and cardboard boxes enter the depot, and are temporarily stacked into provisional arrangements that follow the logic of efficiency and space saving more than of display. However, these groupings equally form a presentation of sorts, one that is equipped with the marks of trajectories and the origins from whence the parts traveled.

Apart from its function as a temporary assembler, the holding room seems to maintain the function of an intermediate space, insofar that it provides a landing as well as another stage setup—hidden from the public—for the art object to arrive to or leave from. Not merely storage, but a passing vessel for transforming the currency of things that travel from their descriptions and insurance documents to their gradual unpacking to art objects that will hopefully settle on their own, more subtle terms.

**DOCU-
MENTATION**

I am thinking about a type of artistic and curatorial approach that has, quite recently, started to put forward and prioritize art objects that are over-indebted to exhibition documentation as their primary mode of being in the world. That is to say, physical work that is envisioned from its outset in the key of measuring up to the lofty standards of High Definition documentation (tiff tiff tiff). It is, in short, work that takes the basic and often human right of reproduction rather literally, and seriously (copy, copy, copy of a copy)—and we, curators, artists, and gallerists alike, believe in the potential of images: to be seen, to travel, and to expand and proliferate freely with their captions.

This shift, through which the pre-Internet brain is overturned, leads one to perceive a seemingly infinite array of exhibitions and spaces, from behind a screen, without the need of relocating oneself "in the flesh" toward "the real." It lays the conditions for a vertical space of reading and viewing exhibitions, in which one documented exhibition is listed after another. A space that equally serves as a swamp of evidence (it did happen, it did take place), in which documentation acknowledges the endeavors of its makers and grants their projects and events with a status of plausibility and truthfulness (picture or it did not happen); indeed, documentation as evidence.

How does this move from "the real" to the work's digitization and online actualization change our understanding of the exhibition vis-à-vis its documentation, which no longer comes after but is already here, as the primary form of engagement? Structurally undermining and bypassing the exhibition as a medium in its own right, we might indeed foresee a movement toward documentation without exhibitions, or, more speculatively, an environment in which exhibitions are staged behind closed doors for documentation purposes only, and thus become publicly inaccessible—akin to the fashion shoot with its stylists, models, and photographer.

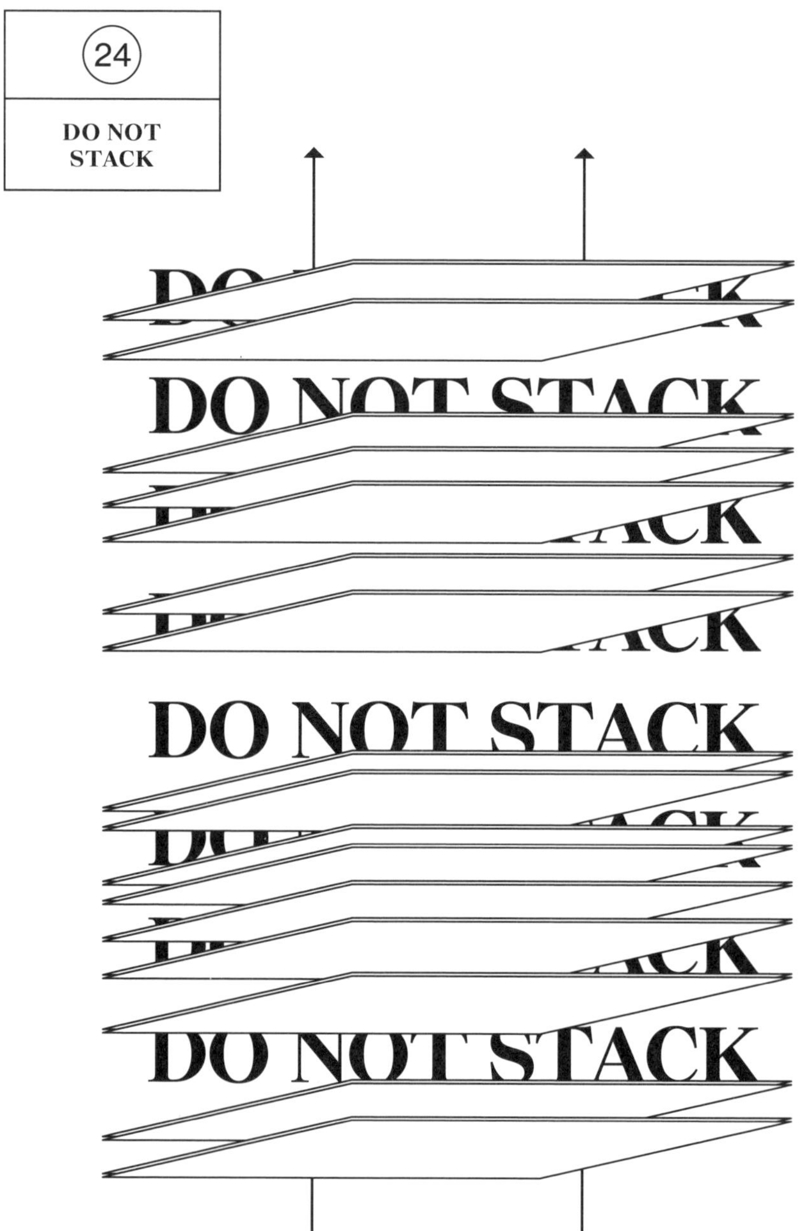
24
DO NOT
STACK
DO NOT STACK
DO NOT STACK
DO NOT STACK
DO NOT STACK

ENCAGEMENT

Somewhere in a dim corner of the exhibition space, in one of those dead-end pockets lacking momentum, hung a 3-meter wide vitrine, suspended midway between ceiling and floor, or, that is to say, at the standard 150 centimeters. As if approaching a lobster, in an aquatic fish tank reminiscent of those in seafood restaurants, the woman halted before the vitrine.[1] Indeed, inspecting a lobster is a rather specific posture for halting, but it is nonetheless apt in describing the way in which the woman observed and looked through the rubble encased within. She might have been looking at one of those slime mold installations by Finnish artist Jenna Sutela, equally fascinating and dystopian in nature, connoting a similar set of transhuman references.

What caught this woman's attention, however, was a yellowish substance resembling something between a large dot of polyurethane foam and an omelet, growing over one of those artificial rock formations often found in aquariums. On closer inspection, the thing was pulsating and seemed to be expanding. Looking into the vitrine, she was overpowered by an eerie and bewildering sensation and became transposed, momentarily transported even. Lured through the glass and submerged into the pulsating thing, she became the life of whatever it was on the other side of the glass—or rather became her not-self in the not-self that was the pulsating thing.[2] Eight hours seemed to condense into a single minute, in which our woman was submerged in the thing that was alternately growing and retreating—producing a gray, crackling, and foaming soundtrack of its own.

But wait. Let us stop tracing the narrative of Julio Cortázar's short story "Axolotl,"[3] which follows a man in his daily visits to the axolotl enclosure at a zoo, where he is entirely consumed by the friendly gaze of the animal and eventually becomes one himself.[4] We were, in fact, talking about slime mold—formerly classified as fungi but no longer considered part of that kingdom—an eukaryotic organism that can live freely as single cells, but that aggregate together to form multicellular reproductive structures.

In contrast to Cortázar's protagonist, the woman in our vitrine became quite wary of her respective place in the scheme of things: indeed, she moved through different states and structures, and had entered into some kind of metamorphic zone in which qualities are exchanged.[5] Being an experienced exhibition visitor herself, she came up with the word "encagement," as a slight variation on the overused utilization of "engagement" in art contexts. She used it as a description of her sensational encounter with a thing seemingly captured and encased. How, in some obscure but mighty real manner, can an encounter with "an unknown and different other" equally give shape to your life's becoming, while remaining bound to the fleshed-existence of the human?[6] "The way to enable each other's stable adaptation over time, is to first of all recognize that the object stares back,"[7] she thought.

1   David Foster Wallace's essay "Consider the Lobster" concerns the ethics of boiling a creature alive in order to enhance consumer pleasure, and includes a discussion of the lobster's sensory neurons. David Foster Wallace, "Consider the Lobster," in *Consider the Lobster – And Other* Essays (New York: Little, Brown and Company and Time Warner Book Group, 2005), 235–55.

2   Aldous Huxley, *The Doors of Perception and Heaven and Hell* (London: Vintage Books, 2004), 19.

3   Julio Cortázar, "Axolotl," in *Blow-Up and Other Stories*, trans. Paul Blackburn (New York: Pantheon Books, 2013), 3–9.

4   Here I recommend an on-line revisiting of curator Sabel Gavaldon's exhibition "Axolotlism"—looking into non-human animals and encounters with radical forms of otherness—at Nogueras-Blanchard Gallery, Madrid, 2015.

5   For a discussion of the "metamorphic" zone, see: Bruno Latour, "Agency at the Time of the Anthropocene," *New Literary History* 45 (2014): 1–18.

6   This is an argument formed by the idea of "becoming in relation to" advanced in *How Forests Think: Toward an Anthropology Beyond the Human* by Eduardo Kohn (Berkeley, Los Angeles, and London: University of California Press, 2013) and the concept of the "fleshed-existence" prompted by Rosi Braidotti in: *The Posthuman* (Cambridge and Malden: Polity Press, 2013).

7   See: James Elkins, *The Object Stares Back: On the Nature of Seeing* (San Diego, New York, and London: Harvest Book, 1997), 46–85.

At the exhibition event, one must be careful not to aestheticize the social, but rather one should aim to socialize the aesthetics of such an occasion and its actors. In other words, perceptual and empirical inclinations may inform a kind of thinking that prefers to tinker with the social dynamics between things and actors—thinking which effectively abandons the transformative capacities of the event. They—the actants—can perform the mattering and relationship-forming on their own behalf, among themselves, but what about the added processes of transformation (events) that spring from these configurations of interacting things and their newly established relations? What is to be found also, in addition to, and as a product of their engagement?

Cooking with dogs might provide you with a convivial situation for preparing a custard pudding. Spending time with a furry dog and its adorable litter gives you adequate reason to produce some documentation for a Snapchat. Best trends forever.

The dog enters the exhibition space without too much difficulty. After having passed the front desk without being detected, it is now lurking around the corner. The other animal exhibition visitors (humans) instantaneously flee upon seeing the dog, seeking refuge on top of plinths and pedestals, where they remain relatively untouched.

After having kept the dog captive for decades, pursuing endless but unsuccessful efforts to impose human meanings and behaviors on the dog, the intentions to turn it into a docile feline companion were eventually abandoned in favor of celebrating the year of online images of cats instead—creating a situation in which the dog's rapid transformation and development as a self-organizing species in the absence of humankind went by completely unnoticed. Upon its sudden and unexpected reappearance, sniffing around one of the plinths, the dog now stands in the cool conceptual shade of the exhibition space, freed from domestic parole, embodying a radical form of otherness, and evoking a feeling of dominance over the human onlookers.

When the differences between pet-hood and object-hood were still indistinct, it was common practice to prepare a dog for an exhibition.[1] For decades, dogs were admired for their outstanding dorsal features. In certain pet exhibits, dogs were rated for how well their appearance conformed to an imposed standard. Dogs did not enjoy these normative ethics, but they understood the frames of civil obedience. Being well aware that adherence to a scheme of common behaviors would never bring forward any vectors of liberation, dogs still maintained the hope of becoming and then entangling with the human-language speaking animal.

The trail from domestic object to abject subject was smooth: the dog never needed humans, the dog only needed humans in captivity. Through a

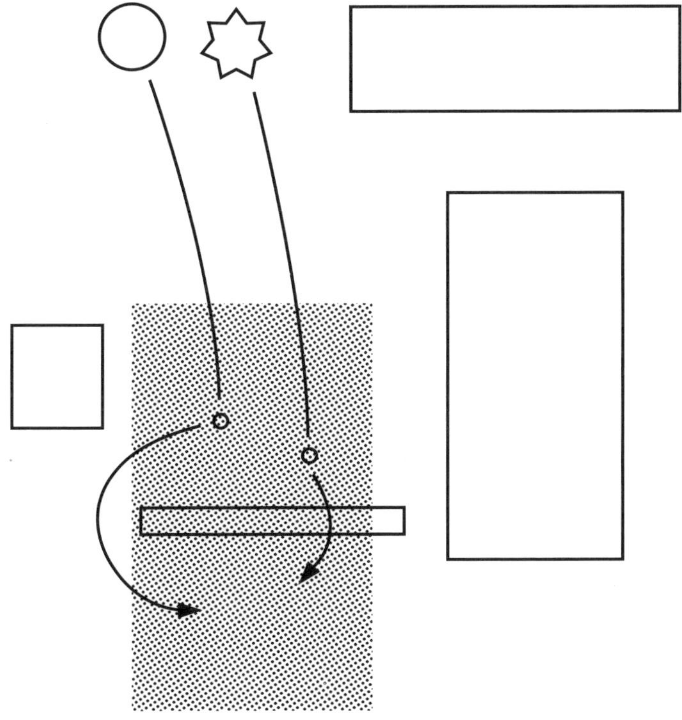

Choreography for one visitor, one dog, and four plinths

process of selective breeding and castration, the dog became a malleable substance upon which the human figure could imprint certain needs, desires, and ideas. At one point it all became slightly too unidirectional for the dog. While humans were resting comfortably in their category of being, the dog set itself adrift.

The dog, still fairly accustomed to the space of an exhibition, enjoys the dynamics of a group show. With no strings attached, and many interactions, relationships, and organisms to account for, the dog tracks the pieces, connects the dots, gazes at the humans on the plinths in this more-than-human, cultivated world. The humans, in turn, are provoked by the dog's destabilizing movement and observation, and the ruptures it imposes on their comfort zones. What *is* the dog looking at, what is it thinking?

1 See, for example: Joseph Beuys, *Coyote* (1974); William Wegman, *Two Dogs and Ball* (1972), *Spelling Lesson* (1973–74), and *Dog Duet* (1975–76); Pierre Huyghe, *Human* (2012); and Krõõt Juurak and Alex Bailey, *Animal Jokes (for Animals)* (2014) and *Performances for Pets* (2014).

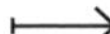

EXHIBITION SPACE

Just as soil counterbalances the carbon dioxide produced by plants, "normal" human behavior and common sense flattens the constructed artificiality of one's surroundings.[1] Here, common sense concerns the protocol of not looking deeper than a certain level, and, instead, facing the world as a reader of surfaces, without thinking through the oddities presented within and beyond the "given-ness" of surfaces and their effects.[2] To act upon the notion of common sense and behavior is to also assume the imperturbable internal self-organization of other objects and entities, to overlook their processes and complexities, and remain in the intermediate and eventful space of surfaces.[3]

From this standpoint, the principle architectural features of the exhibition space — floor, ceiling, and walls — could be considered as measurements toward establishing a state of normality, as attempts to construct an autonomous world that is set apart and held in stasis. An architecture of horizontal and vertical volumes erected to keep what is undesired from entering into the frame — among, for instance, the acid architecture of the air — while simultaneously informing and negotiating a set of normal behaviors through acts of designating surfaces for convenient viewing experiences. In so doing, the exhibition space becomes a spatiotemporal vacuum, or, perhaps, somewhat of a self-referential continuum. For instance, treading on concrete slabs resting on unseen and foundational layers of rudimentary material is to act on an actively operating exclusion mechanism. Hence, fields of vision and lines of sight are—by necessity—made limited to gear toward a specific reading of interior surfaces. Then, to take the exhibition floor is to, hopefully, knowingly and willingly accept that the seemingly solid foundations and surroundings of the exhibition space function as a construct that extols some scales of time and space above others. In turn, the awareness of this layered and constructed setup may trigger an awareness that the outside world, and the various material registers, life forms, and interrelations that it hosts, is actively talking back to you through the space of an exhibition, and through your encounter with an art object.[4] In other words: it is possible to be outside of an exhibition by means of an exhibition.[5] Allowing one to think about an external substance, context, or force by means of having an encounter with something else first,[6] the space and time of an exhibition can indeed effectively expand the continuum of life elsewhere.

1   Text paraphrased from: Gwenneth Boelens and Nickel van Duijvenboden, "The Retained," in *Il Faut* (self-published, 2006).

2   Ibid.

3   This argument is put forward in: Graham Harman, *The Quadruple Object* (Winchester and Washington: Zero Books, 2011), 24–7.

4   The definition of art as an agent that makes "the world talk back to you," is from: Chus Martínez, "The Octopus in Love," *e-flux journal* 55 (2014), http://www.e-flux.com/journal/the-octopus-in-love.

5   In the documentation series *L'Abécédaire de Gilles Deleuze* (1988–89), philosopher Gilles Deleuze speaks about the responses he received to his book *The Fold: Leibnitz and the Baroque* (1988, published in English in 1993). Deleuze received a letter from a surfer who wrote about how he rides and dissects waves, and reacts to the folds they provide. The surfer's words allowed Deleuze, in turn, to exemplify the idea of "going outside of philosophy by means of philosophy," to detour and to let this "outside" inform his practice. In the frame of an exhibition, this thought is particularly pertinent to thinking about the exhibition as an assembling ground, even as an ecology of sorts, that enables us to come to terms with the external influences that inform our daily living and working practices.

6   Paraphrased from the protagonist in Jean-Luc Godard's film *In Praise of Love* (2001).

FILLER

To maintain the image of a smooth transition from exhibition to exhibition, the doors of the exhibition space are temporarily closed. Visitors are notified by a Post-it on the door that gently locks them out via a cryptic mentioning of "Installation in progress. Opening on August 18." On the inside, staff members are privy to the mess, the sleepless nights, the moving of crates to recreate space, and the horrors of a lost remote control eventually found next to an empty pizza box.

Each time, the install situation calls for decomposition and reconstruction, as the preceding exhibition and its constituents—especially those in need of anchoring—have left their marks and traces. In the process of renovating one scenario toward the building of another, labor is distributed among the group, in correspondence with the positions taken and the skill sets available. Designated members of the team are applying filler: a smooth white paste, often provided in small plastic buckets, that is used to cover holes and cracks in the wall, often aided by a palette knife, a sponge, a finger. Once applied, the soft material will harden to recreate the stable image of a seemingly unused wall. Filler is the primer for the staging of many exhibitions. It could be posited that filler is mainly applied to spaces with a history of consecutive exhibitions that are inclined to refuse to show the physical traces of their previous efforts. In rendering marks of the past invisible, a particular component of the history of exhibitions—and the institutional archive—is detached from the space itself and must be translated and vocalized through speech acts.

In this particular case, filler is employed as an instrument for erasure, employed to prioritize what is happening in the present, and to answer the call of contemporary art's continuous need for renewal. Here the smooth and seemingly untouched blank wall is prioritized as a placeholder: a clean surface for the positioning and the placement of works anew. To maintain these smooth surfaces for spatial inscription, filler is used as a tool for spatial resurgence—applied, smoothed with sandpaper, and dabbed with paint in time for the opening act—to effectively remove ambiguous and

patchy areas stained by previous events. A device of shifting constitution that instead of being sought to probe for an essence on the inside, is put forward in flattening and filling out on the level of the surface, *ad infinitum.*

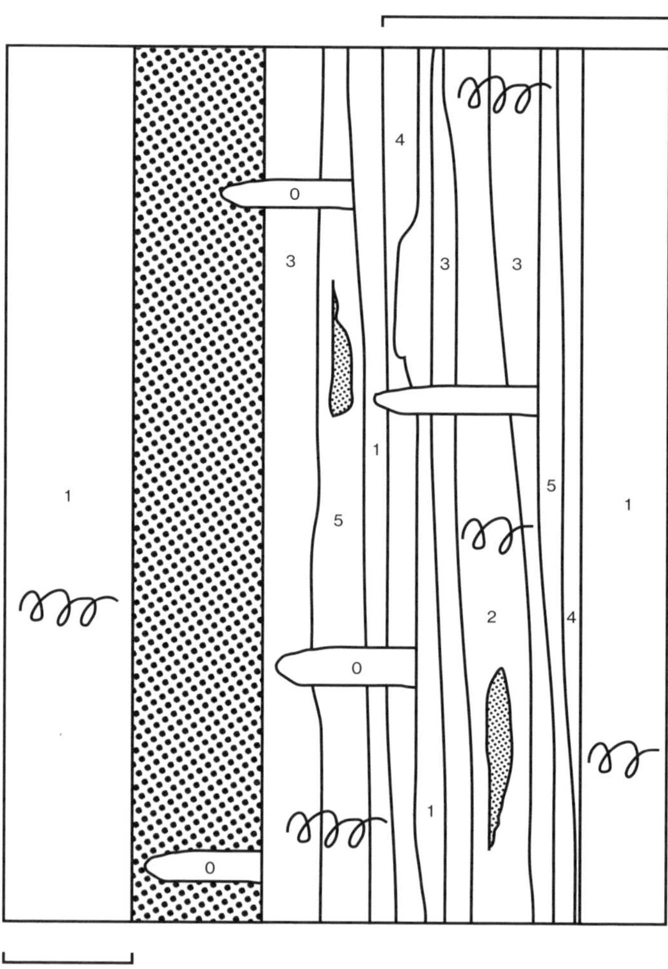

FLOOD

What started as a seemingly controlled leak, caused by a water pipe suffering from material fatigue, soon resulted in a general collapse of the institutional base. After a few drops of water hit a visitor's head, measurements were taken by suspending a shallow collecting tray from the ceiling. The liquid's intervals were calibrated, and, in step with the institution's maintenance tempo, the accumulated water was discarded on Monday mornings.

Matters worsened with a change in season, which heralded a greater intensity in rainfall. However, the deteriorating situation failed to prompt any adjustment to the container, even though the ceiling attachments were only able to hold a certain volume and weight. The container spilled over occasionally, leaving a yellow tinted relief on the floor, and the small currents of water, finding their way from the ceiling, started to defy the laws of gravity and the institutional tray-management routine. Small indentations and grooves were carved out by the persistent streams, which not only enlarged the hole in the ceiling, but also left increasingly large puddles on the floor.

During the night of August 30 the heaviest rainfall since 1906 occurred, with an average precipitation of 680 millimeters. What would have previously been considered as a notable but small hole increased into a significant point of entry. With a hole large enough to let in wildlife, the outside had started leaking into the exhibition space.

Attempts to overcome the breach began with one staff member trying to establish an overview from the elevated points of the exhibition space. Overlooking the grand hall, one could observe a large and seemingly artificial indoor lake, adorned with dry shorelines on the sides where floor levels proved to be higher. With the water rising to around 62 centimeters, one could spot an archipelago of firmly secured plinths in the near distance, almost like the foundation piles for an offshore drilling platform. One of the fluorescent lights was flickering and, through contact with the open wires in the central fuse box, the pooled water was live. The space had

Flood (or: one ecosystem taking over another)

Unknown artist
2016–17

Debris, epoxy, mold, rust, rainwater, mud, live animals, butterflies, fungi on plinths, puddles, leakage, acid-free paper, wind, various birds, free-floating exhibition catalogs, oil, acrylic and elements on canvas, (de)humidifier, plants

With sp… …ral impo…
in …tu…

turned into a swamp—things floated around, the water was dotted with debris, some epoxy sculptures drifted while others protruded slightly above water level.

As soon as the electricity was fixed and the water was drained, a troupe of conservators and cleaning staff were released into the space. Marching through the rubble, the conservators started making marks in their notebooks, working toward a preliminary condition report of the situation. The environment—one overcome by a rupture, a natural disaster of sorts—was clearly marked by a general state of *unexhibitability,* at least from the perspective of the conservators. In actual fact, the scene had a tranquil ambiance, and while some entities resisted, others were quietly enjoying the environmental shifts, and it had become increasingly difficult to discern between what was art, no-longer-art, and never-considered-to-be-art. Since most of the artists participating in the now-swamped exhibition had abandoned pictorial regimes and craft in favor of industrial materials such as powder-coated steel, sheets of neon Plexiglas, and aluminum rods, the conservators had to begin the difficult task of sorting between those things thought of as artist-made, and those considered to be standard construction materials or equipment.

Objects were rapidly deteriorating, deforming, and turning into hybrid constellations of intertwined materialities, so the team rushed to establish an orderly classification system that could be unanimously and quickly agreed upon. Some art objects had disappeared entirely, leaving behind only vague traces of their previous states. In trying to move beyond this mayhem, this unclassifiable zombie formalist soup, the decision to normalize the situation arrived in a timely manner with a press release statement from the institution saying: "The life force could simply not be contained any longer."

<table>
<tr><td>(31)</td></tr>
<tr><td>**FLOOR PLAN**</td></tr>
</table>

As an improvised form of cartography, the exhibition floor plan could perhaps be considered as an abstract and cryptic visual language. In the process of making a floor plan, by allocating abstracted forms and shapes to stand in for and represent onsite physicalities, we are confronted with a shift in perspective and dimension, marked by a projection of architectural outlines and elements of the exhibition space onto a two-dimensional plane. A second move involves scaling and translating: in facing the floor plan, we are seeing the exhibition from above. Inasmuch as this bird's-eye view could be considered a spoiler for what is to come, what is about to be seen, it might as well be considered as a convenient mode of human-scale representation in a workable, still, rigid, and hand-held format; a scale model of the exhibition presented as a congruent, single whole. Yet another translation takes place in the field of perception: the more or less frontal encounter with objects and entities in the actual exhibition space is countered by the floor plan's flat approximation of their shape and outline from above. Paintings, shelves, and temporary walls become lines, monitors become black squares or rectangles, and the difference between sculptures, installations, and tables are expressed by flat depictions of variable lengths and widths, with possible slight variations of the color and saturation of the substitute shape. This swarm of graphic elements is then suffused with symbols, numbers, and designations that link the visual components to their associated textual information: their makers, titles, years of production, media, dimensions, durations, and so on. Culminating in a static visual and textual analogy, the floor plan is a crypto-language conceived for the spatiality and thinking of human beings, a type of concrete poetry that functions both as a tool for navigation and as a document that may later, after the exhibition closes, be considered as a remnant of a past choreography or constellation.

FLUORESCENT LIGHT

Upon walking into the exhibition space, after passing the reception desk and the cloakroom, one is struck by a feeling of hyper awareness and an awkward silence not uncommon during dinners hosted by distant relatives. This feeling applies to everybody, although the more seasoned visitor will likely be accustomed to the required evasive maneuver: acting casual and pretending to look at things while generally scoping out the space to obtain an overview.

One of the main fixtures that is key in instigating this initial feeling of uneasiness and turning the exhibition into an investigative *Exhibit A* is the fluorescent light. You, the visitor, become subjected to an almost surgical and directionless whiteness distributed everywhere by a relentless flood of fluorescent light bouncing toward and submerging you. Here, however, many points of view are kept in suspension, and, for a while at least, the shifting degrees of uncertainty as to the subject of interrogation are maintained. While you were thinking that *you* were being placed under scrutiny, in your overly self-conscious state, you happen to misread the intentions of the fluorescent lights. Did you have something to say? Were you expecting to be part of the plot? You were wrong. The fluorescent light operates under the democratic principle of not prioritizing any one thing: an even distribution of illumination means that all the objects are prioritized equally and are allowed to speak simultaneously. Welcome! Now that you have been cleared of your anticipated exhibitionism, the mood is not exactly somber, and all matters are at least on the same footing.

33

FRAGILE

FRAGILE
FRAGILE
FRAGILE
FRAGILE
FRAGILE

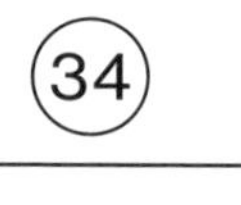

GLOVES

Overcome by an urge to sift through and browse what is at hand—a childlike desire to move from passive observer to active participant—your hand slips into a second skin. Once your fingers reach the tips of the one-size-fits-all cotton glove, you obtain your right of passage. Is this an act of motor self-censorship, a means of adhering to an imposed rule set tacitly but effectively voiced by the institution against the public degradation of its contents? Or perhaps it is a more fetishistic pleasure as part of a prolonged archival fever that spurns this buffer zone between the index finger and the materials at hand?

As a newly formed and curious apparatus, the glove is contractually bound with the hand as an intermediate agent that somewhat numbs the nerve terminals and limits sensation, while enabling the surface of the encapsulated skin tissue to access the surface of the object. As the arbiter of non-existent surface effects—although the glove is accountable for a fair share of the dirty work—one's intellect is now more nourished via a perceptual circuitry, the glove having effectively numbed part of the sensorium by excluding the sense of touch. Within this maneuver, one might understand the paradox of the "hand in glove" as describing intimate and proximate relationship with the object of access while simultaneously becoming a sensation of its own.

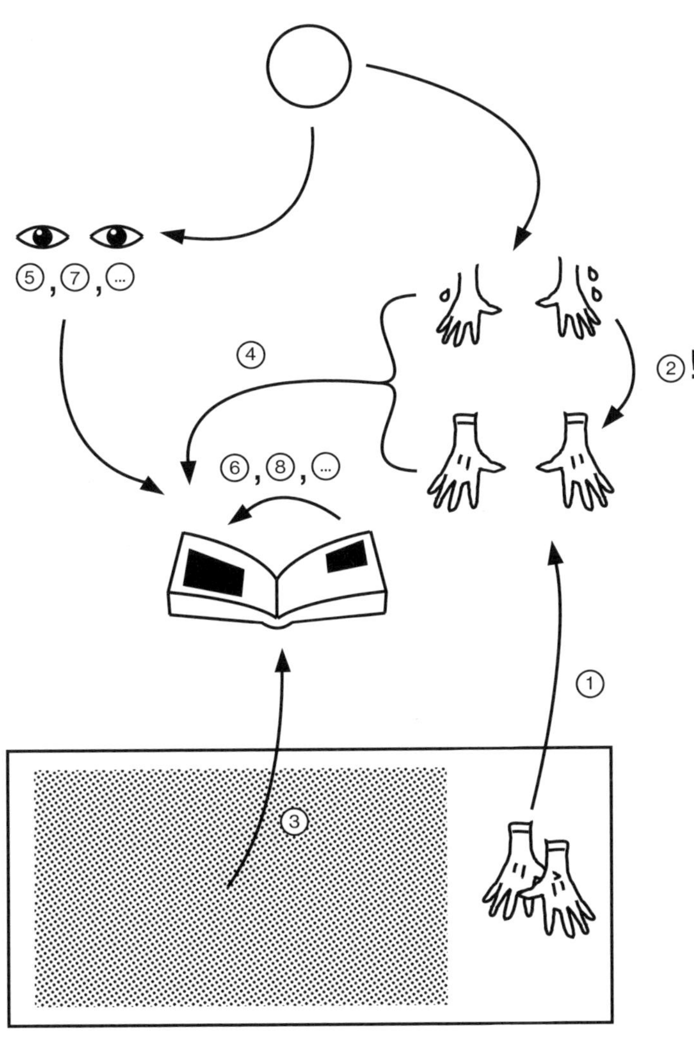
(5),(7),...
(4)
(2)!
(6),(8),...
(1)
(3)

<table>
<tr><td>(35)

GUIDED TOUR</td><td>Dear person, welcome to our pack. You are the last to join, but not to worry, I will be your guiding principle. There is no need for you to lead the way, you just have to adhere to our formation and its movements, indicated by me, your host and exhibition guide. For a</td></tr>
</table>

given duration, let us say between half an hour and an hour, for the sake of brevity, we will form a close-knit group. As such, we are all equally bound to a certain sense of contractual obligation and commitment, provided that you willingly entered into this agreement with me, your peers, and the narrative arc of the tour.

Essentially, for the duration of our time together, we are collectively cloaked *en masse* until the words "thank you for attending this guided tour" are spoken, at which point the active workings of our gathering will dissolve. Bystanders can feign to be in alignment with the pack, but will never become full members, as they were absent from the group's initiation rite. You will remain aware of this unequal footing until the infiltrating attendees have left your field of vision. To break the spell from within is also to systematically disrupt and undermine the imposed order of coherence and the collective spirit. Although do feel free to leave at any time, or ask questions.

OK. Let us start. You might have been drawn to this guided tour with an urgency of "wanting to know more about the exhibition," or perhaps already knowing, but wanting to hear it again, hear it better, or to prepare to outsmart me afterward. You might equally have been encouraged by a sense of curiosity triggered by a staff member or a friend.

These desires are easily gratified, so much so that many of your fellow tour members go into hibernation mode after a mere six minutes. Instead of being attentive to the tour, they become disconnected, and grow increasingly conscious of themselves and their surroundings, their hairdo, the need to clip their nails, the effort another member has made on their makeup or in matching their socks.

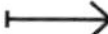

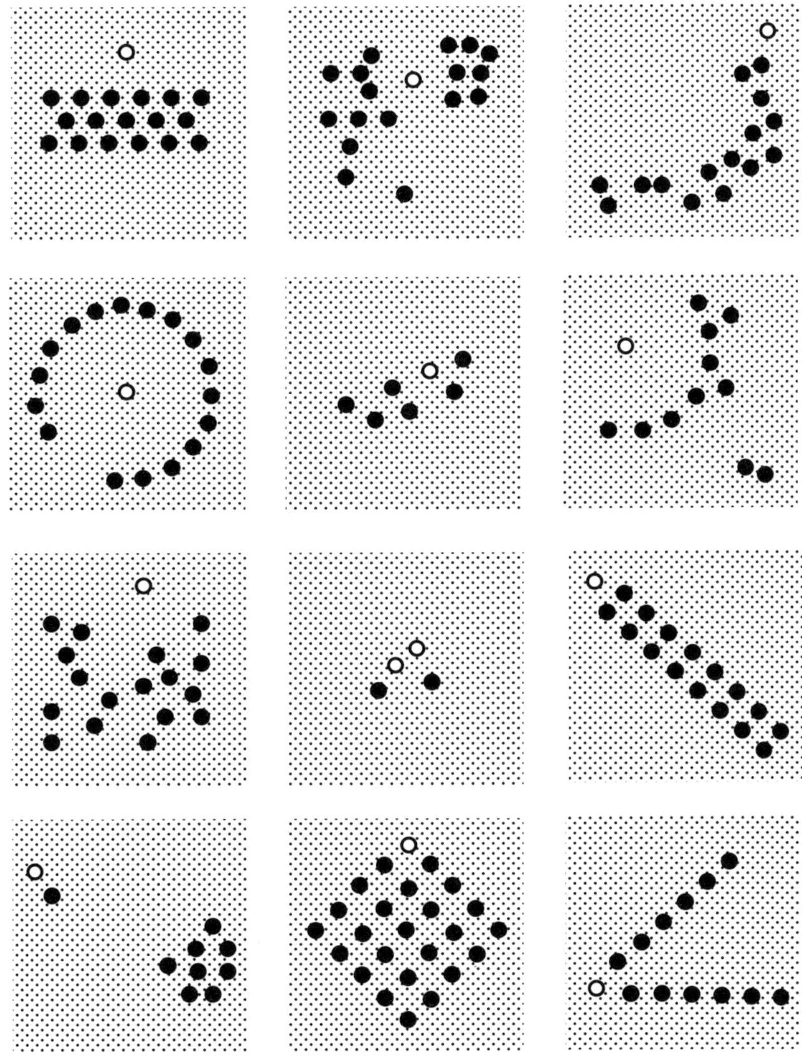

Guided-tour formations I-XII

At a later stage in the tour, the vague contours of readily existing factions and partitions within the group start to manifest themselves more boldly: we are not one, we are two, and more. My increasingly intensifying speech starts to amplify the silence of the tour followers in such a way that my pauses become loaded with an eerie sensation of the absent social cohesion of our group.

We halt at certain points within the space, in the proximity of art objects. "Frankly, that's quite interesting. I could never have thought of it myself," you may quip. This remark forms a fundamental goal of the guided tour: my studies of a given text, which often constitute active and often short-term knowledge, are translated into a message conveyed, pronounced, and delivered with a cadence of confidence and complete dedication, in relation to your unthinking. I am a conveyer of imposed knowledge that I only preside over in a partial manner, which I gradually feed into your space and your auditory channels, and which forms an even more partial and fragmented memory for you.

THANK YOU
FOR ATTENDING
THIS TOUR.
AS YOU BEGIN
TO FREELY DISPERSE
THROUGHOUT
THE EXHIBITION,
THIS TOUR WILL
AUTO-DESTRUCT
AFTER TWO MINUTES
OF CONTEMPLATION.

(36)

HANDLE WITH CARE

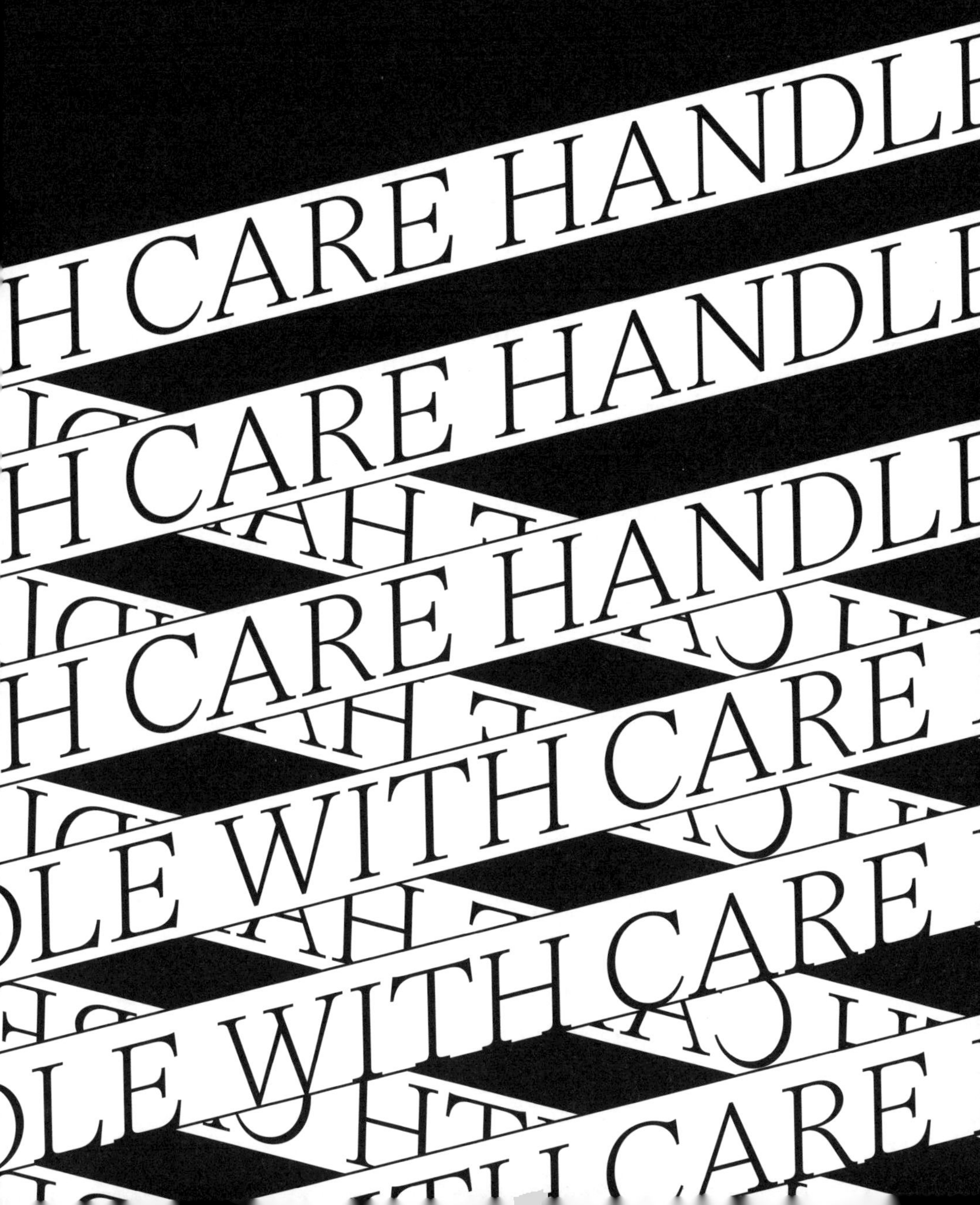
H CARE HANDLE
H CARE HANDLE
H CARE HANDLE
DLE WITH CARE
DLE WITH CARE

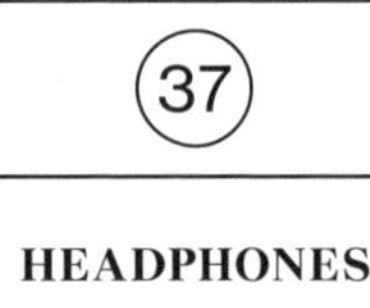

A two-channel monologue
for two actors.

A   —Where did the wireless headphones go?

B   —You came across a pair of headphones in the exhibition. You put them on, and suddenly found yourself in
close proximity to the work, as dictated by the length
of the cable, which in turn established a certain intimacy
between you and the art object.

A   —Hold on. This set of headphones was attached to a
monitor playing a video. One set was found on the monitor, the other on the stool in front of the monitor.

A   —In any case, "By listening on headphones, visitors are
offered a new level of perception which leads from the
conventionally visual approach to artworks toward an
auditory, more imaginative experience, offering scope
for different mental visualizations," the woman from the
communications department said.

B   —The unseasoned listener tends to ignore the presence
of the sound on their headphones and speaks to their
companion with a raised voice.

A   —Now, those people over there, the two wearing head
phones, what are they doing?

A   —I had not fully prepared this question. I just asked it out loud because I could not hear myself properly.

B   —You want to listen first and see second?

A   —What is the relationship between the sound and the image?

B   —Translation.

A   —Time passes, the voice disappears.

A   —You wonder where you will end up next. Another track, another seat, a different voice.

B   —In the end you become aware that you have been part of a conspiracy between curator and work: the curator had to compromise due to her desire to program so many sound works in a single space.

HUMANS

If we think of the exhibition space as a spatiotemporal ecology in which a constellation of autonomous objects is put forward as an event that we have come to know as an "exhibition," how should the human figure, in their short-term cohabitation with other constituent objects, be approached? And what could the differences provoked by the sudden manifestation of the human to the exhibition objects consist of?

I am not referring to a sudden renegotiation that would leave all the difference-making to humans and the triggers for perception-making to the objects, as both entities possess these qualities, and exchange them in each other's mutual proximity. Rather, I want to consider the shifts in the qualities of a human being that occur when their shape-changing capacities are transposed and applied to a local manifestation, that is, in this instance, the exhibition space as a metamorphic zone.[1]

In paraphrasing Levi R. Bryant, let us think of human beings as rogue objects: as objects that are not chained to any given assemblage of objects, but instead wander in and out of assemblages, modifying relations as they go.[2] This is not to say, by any means, that the being and physical constitution of the object in the exhibition space is exhausted, changed, or altered by the human figure putting itself forward. Rather, the human being is capable of bearing and forging new relations within the exhibition constellation that challenge and change the normative and scripted space of the exhibition and its contents, and can equally preside over the possibility of acting on its own account, becoming both integral to and externalizing itself from the exhibition assemblage.

←

1 The "metamorphic zone" is Bruno Latour's term from "How Better to Register the Agency of Things" (lecture, Tanner Lectures, Yale University, Yale, March 26–27, 2014), published online at: http://www.bruno-latour.fr/node/563: "But on what I have proposed to call the metamorphic zone where humans and non-humans keep exchanging their properties, that is, their figurations. A non-anthropomorphic character is a character all the same. It has agency. It moves. It undergoes trials. It elicits reactions. It becomes describable. This, however, does not mean that we are 'projecting' anthropomorphic features on what should remain an object: it simply means that the shape, that is, the morphism of the human character is just as open to inquiry, to shape-changing, as that of a non-human. Put more bluntly, it means that the older philosophical tools of object and subject are wholly inadequate to follow the many descriptions, the many accounts that are pouring out of our scriptoria—be they laboratories, offices, studios or libraries. Here, something else is at work, has always been at work, something that does modify the shapes of whichever ingredient you throw inside, much like a fiercely boiling sorcerers' cauldron."

2 Levi R. Bryant, *Onto-Cartography: An Ontology of Machines and Media* (Edinburgh: Edinburgh University Press, 2014), 208.

<table>
<tr><td>(39)

INSTALLATION PERIOD</td><td>Looking to find a situation that combines the most diverse number of exchanges and intensities between actors and agendas, the installation period would certainly rank among the most inward-looking and complex of material and fleshed choreographies. A</td></tr>
</table>

variation on a Fluxus ballet—performed exclusively for and by those select members of the troupe—during an installation period the institution's surface is temporarily paused, whereas the inside is pulsating and vibrating with activity. Brimming with anticipation, the installation period takes the shape of an intermediate zone, an incubation period granted with transformative powers of organic reshuffling that leads the institutional body into a new life cycle. This cycle is partially preconceived and designed, insofar as sketches, floor plans, and spatial concepts are placed on the translation table and trickle into the exhibition spaces for their timely realization: from the offices, the curators' desks, and the mailboxes, into the hands of the manufacturers, technicians, and art handlers. Prior negotiations are put to the test of material durability and diplomacy—will it hold, stand, rise, cohabit, tolerate, and expand, spatially, textually, and conceptually, all at once? Most importantly, the installation period is foremost a time of "becoming," one that is clearly underpinned and necessitated by a sense of "arriving."

Within this brief and linear semi-private affair, one is able to observe sets and subsets of relationships acting out, under the guiding auspices of proprietors and troubleshooters. From station to station, paths are carved through material volumes, timescales, things, and peoples that exchange positions and take on wholly different roles day by day. At one station, we find an artist sitting next to an installation that was abandoned temporarily in favor of an unexpected and urgent technical deadlock; elsewhere, just before the entrance of the exhibition space, we encounter a construction table with several tape measures, a spirit level, box cutter, empty battery packaging, sawdust, and cable ties, interspersed with a leftover lunch scenario, of which lukewarm coffee in paper cups, creamer, breadcrumbs, and packages of processed meats remain. Close by, a dark-gray wall that previously served as the backdrop for a video projection is receiving its first white latex coat and the marketer posts an image of an artist unpacking

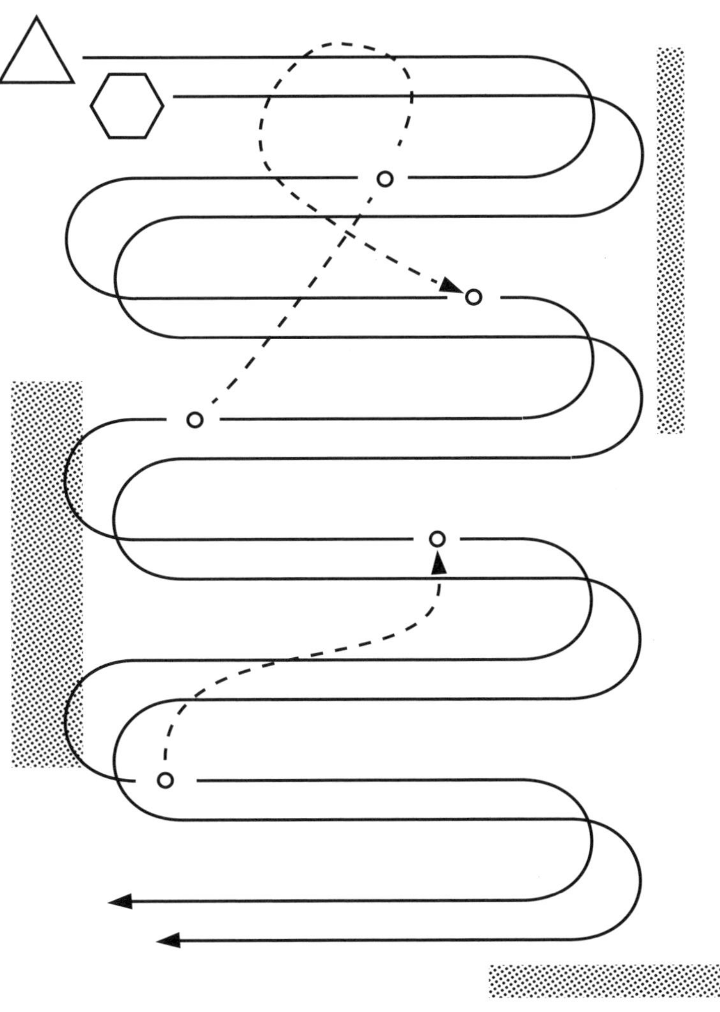

Choreography for one curator and one broom, to be performed in the last
ten minutes before the exhibition opens (with possible improvisations)

her powder-coated steel rods from crates, amounting to an instant pool of likes—the reassembling of a work is a favorable, publically sharable midpoint in the installation process. Another station hosts a number of art objects protected by their Bubble Wrap; empty cardboard boxes, sheets of plastic, and wads of crumpled tape tumble through the space; one artist's peers who happen to be in the vicinity drop by, effectively delaying the discussion with an installer about using some different spotlights. Elsewhere, the remaining clutter is being shoveled into dustbins or stuffed into storage rooms; the intermediate state steadily morphing into speeches, mounted wall labels, and elevator pitches. A tipping point passed, another wave in the making.

A modular and fleeting entity, made of flesh-toned clay. Characterized by readiness and flexibility, the intern mutates in response to sets of prescribed tasks and curriculums, as it well understands that adaptation is key to survival.

Rather unexpectedly, the intern arrives at the doorstep of the institution on a given morning, introduces itself, and proffers its labor in the exhibition space in return for the reimbursement of travel costs. Soon one remembers the brief interview that followed a "Call for Interns," which was answered by 300 applications from MFA, MA, and PhD students.

As newborns to a readily saturated market of cognitive workers, those interns who have obtained "intern status" before, proactive as they might seem to be, rarely appear to take flight, often remaining within the feedback loop of internship after internship. This plague might be overturned by marking the Chinese zodiac with the addition of "The Year of the Intern." Wishful thinking, yes.

For three to six months, the intern is overcome by occasional gusts of Stockholm syndrome, developing odd sympathies for—in an act of self-legitimation, and as to delay a nervous breakdown—the respective institution, and the general negligence imposed by its members. Simultaneously, the intern might be mistaken for a curator by a member of the public, upon which it might method-act itself into the role, being perfectly aware of the required traits and behavioral patterns. At other times, the intern can be found in the archive, the attic, at the liquor store, performing all the tasks it has mostly invented itself—having made (justified) projections about being an indispensable tool in the day-to-day operation of the institute.

Here it seems befitting to note that the intern is a valuable asset to the subsistence of institutions and the enhancement of their internal self-organization. Whereas, perhaps rather paradoxically so, the figure of the intern is often framed as an investment on the level of the respective institute,

a time-consuming burden, adopted as part of an institutional sense of responsibility toward developing talent, and enhancing skills and knowledgeability through "hands-on experience" and "working in a lively environment." However, the extent to which the intern's activities go beyond the bar of what any legal definition of an internship would lawfully allow is quite commonly overlooked; silently treating them as coworkers, at least in terms of responsibility and workload, but never acknowledging them as such: "I will not give you full credit, but I am not going to flunk you either."

Let us send the intern out…

The label went on vacation, and thus the art object was left without its accompaniment to summarize—preferably in no more than 200 words—what it stood for. Were it able to speak and be understood in human language, or, conversely, if humans could grapple with its seemingly tacit but no less meaningful speech, both the art object and the label would have said exactly the same thing. The art object was a keen critic of its own being, indeed, it was of a self-reflexive nature and actively engaged in an awareness of its place in the scheme of things, in an exhibition, where it happened to be. A positionality that was not left unnoticed by the label that had implemented itself between the various stakeholders to overcome, or perhaps bypass, the chiasmic logic between things and words—whereas the art object had no intention whatsoever to stand in the cool conceptual shade of the label.

This dynamic had led to numerous conflicts, in which the art object had claimed "language kills the matter," upon which the label commented "it [the art object] has to hinge on its translation into text—be it theoretical, academic, or visitor-friendly—in order to reach out and allow for itself to be understood, properly understood." Matters worsened and many discussions followed, covering such topics as the benefits of pretense and being pretentious, the many discrepancies between surplus, value, and surplus value (let alone the utterly sensitive and thus untouched cases of the user and its exchange value), stiff independence and unnecessary reliance, the objectification of the object, that in turn claimed to be its own subject, and, finally, on learning via didactic mechanisms and self-realization through applying and subjecting oneself to the world.

It would have been beautiful if the label had come to conclude that, indeed, its functionality of consolidating meaning was of a truly nonsensical nature. But, instead, it begged to differ, again and again, to the point at which it abruptly affixed itself to the art object with a staple. Were it not that the art object seemed so utterly indefinable that it appeared to need the textual additions that came with the act of labeling and etiquette, it

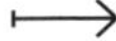

would in fact have actively resisted further description and interpretation. However, the label did not adhere and soon the art object was surrounded by various etiquettes that smoothly glided off its surface. The label then decided to take a spell, but not before partially reconstituting itself as an essay pasted to the wall next to the art object, always following but never quite approximating the subjectivity of its neighboring object.

<table>
<tr><td>The quick brown fox jumps over the lazy artist</td></tr>
<tr><td>Unknown artist
2016–17</td></tr>
<tr><td>Acrylic, books, concrete, digital print on cotton, epoxy, felt, glass (engraved), hardboard, institutionalized organisms, jigsaw piece, knife, lacquer, mixed materials, neon sign, oil (on paper), paper, quartz (mined by the artist), ruler, screen-printed and powder-coated steel, tape, unfired clay, vinyl, wood (oak, MDF), Xerox print on perforated office paper, yeast, zinc</td></tr>
<tr><td></td></tr>
</table>

MARKETING TOOLS

Opening the toolbox of the marketer, we uncover several mouthpieces for an exhibition and its contents. But none of these pieces seem to fit properly. Air spills out from the sides. From the remaining whispers one can distill, quite unexpectedly, a rather clear message, almost entirely transparent even. This message serves as an ongoing pressure performed in the instant abbreviation of exhibition projects. In whose favor does the marketer market? Let us call it a "demographic" for the time being. The marketer is in charge of the perception-making and awareness-raising for an event or exhibition, reaching out to a demographic through a large variety of additional perceptual events and promotional formats. In other words, the marketer boasts the tools to create potential anticipation. The marketer—or communication officer, as they are sometimes called—is also simultaneously a mouthpiece for the demographic they target, having visited their highly local environs in order to acquire insights into the behavioral patterns, mores, and language phenomena that hold the collective together. On return, he or she will possess vital hands-on knowledge to translate the exhibition into products and services for a demographic. For the benefit of the exhibition, I foresee the formation of a language that accounts for the noise in any given reality, by inventing (not finding) its demographic in the rubble and debris on site. Perception is key; now let us try to find the right angle to open the exhibition. There is a logic to be changed.

43 — MEDIA PLAYER

Column 1: aec, amc, am7, am2, amv, apz, aqt, arf, asf, ask, ast, asx, aut, avb, avc, avf, avi, avr, awlive, badongo, bay, bbv, bdav, bdm, bdmv, bdtp, bik, bix, biz, bmk, bnk, box, bsf, bs4, bu, bub, bup, bvr, bvz, bts, cam, camproj, camrec, cct, cin, cine, cip, clpi, cmproj, cpk, crec, ctd, c2r, cvc, cx3, dash, dat, dav, dce, dc8, dcf, demo, demo4

Column 2: dfxp, dif, dir, divx, djanimations, dlx, dmb, dmsd, dmsm, dmss, dmv, dmx, dof, dpd, dpg, dscf, dsm, dtv, d2v, dv, dv-avi, dvddata, dvdmedia, dvdrip, dv4, dv5, dvm, dvr, dvr-ms, dvsd, dvt, dvx, dwz, dxa, dxr, epj, epm, es3, eti, etrg, eva, evo, ev2, exo, eye, ezp, eztv, fbr, fcp, fcpxml, f4v, film, flc, flexolibrary, flh, fli, fli_, flic, flm, flux, flv, flvat, fm2

Column 3: fmv, fpb, fr, fsv, fvt, 4xm, gfp, gifv, gir, gmm, gmt, grasp, g64, gts, gvi, gxf, hav, hdmov, hevc, hgd, hiv, hkv, hmt, hmv, hnm, h64, htd, h260, h261, h.263, h263, h263+, h264, h4v, h265, htp, h3r, hup, ifv, iis, ilm, imovieevent, imovieproj, imovieproject, ipr, irec, irf, irv, isf, ismv, isproj, iva, ivf, iv, ivr, ivs, ivu, jmf, jmm, jpv, jts, jtv, jyk, kmv, k3g, kux, lsx, l3, l32, lza, mb4, mcf, mcv, met

Column 4: m4e, m4f, m4v, m4u, mfp, mfv, mhg, mgv, m-jpeg, mjp, mjpeg, mjpg, mjp2, mj2, mkv3D, ml20, mk3d, mkv, mks, ml20, mmm, mmp, mmv, mnv, mod, moff, moo, moov, m1s, mov, m1v, movie, mpcpl, mpe, mpeg, mpeg1, mpeg2, mpeg4, mp4, mp4v, mp4;v=1, mpg, mpg2, mpg4, mpgv, mpgx, mpj, mps, mp7, mp2v, mpv, mpv2, mrd, mqv, mswmm, m2p, mts, m65, m2s, mts1, m2t, m2ts, m2v, mtv, mv, mvc, mvd, mvf, mv1, mv4, mvp, mvr, mvv, mvw

Column 5: mvy, mxf, mxm, mxv, ncor, nde, nmm, noa, n3r, nut, nuv, nvc, nvl, nxv, ogm, ogv, ogx, otrkey, par, pds, pmf, pmp, ppj, ppp, prel, pro, prproj, p2, pvr, px, pxm, pxv, pyv, qmx, qt, qtc, qtvr, qvt, ratDVD, ravi, rax, rca, rcproject, rdg, rdt, rec, rec_part0, rec_part1, rec_part2, rki, rm, rmvb, roq, rpl, r3d, rt4, rts, rtsp, rtv, rv, rvid, rvl, san, sbst, sce, scm, scn, scr, sdr2, sdv, sec, seq, sfvidcap, siv

Column 6: sky, slc, smv, snapfireshow, snd, sol, sqf, sqz, ssif, ssm, ssw, st4, stk, str, strg, stu, stx, svcd, svd, svi, swc, swf, swi, swt, swz, 60d, tdt2, 3gp, 3gp_128x96, 3gpp, 3gpp2, 3gp2, 3gt, tgv, theater, thp, tivo, tix, tmf, tmi, 3mm, tod, tp, tpd, tp0, trec, TriDefMovie, trn, trp, trt, ts, ts4, tstream, tts, tv, tvs, tvv, ty, tx3g, ub1, urc, usm, uvf, uvs, uvseg, vbc, vcd, vcl, vcm, vc1, vcr, vdf, vdm, vd3

Column 7: veg, vep, vep4, vf, vfo, vg, vghd, vgx, vgz, vid, video, viewlet, viv, vivo, vmif, vmm, vob, vod, vpd, vp8, vpg, vpj, vprj, vproj, vp3, vp6, vro, vse, vs2, vs4, v264, vvf, webm, wm, wm3, wmv, wmv3, wot, wpe, wp3, wsa, w3d, w32, wtv, wve, xas, xavc, xba, xlmv, xmm, xmv, xtodvd, xvid, xp4, xvw, xwmv, yfm, yifj, zeg, 032, 44, 261, 263, 264, 265, 603, 800, 890

MONITOR

An abbreviated biography of the manifold lives of the Hantarex monitor.

In the cold winter of 1945, Ugo Meoni registered his company Hantarex S.p.A. in Florence. Initially producing radios, the company started to manufacture television sets from 1952 onward. Only in the 1970s, during which time Ugo's son Luciano became the CEO of Hantarex, did the company produce its first monitor: "The Hantarex." This was in 1977.[1] Despite its good market position, Hantarex S.p.A. was declared bankrupt in 1995.[2] Following the bankruptcy, Luciano was imprisoned for tax evasion and carousel fraud.

On the basis of its angular, almost cubical shape, the Hantarex was initially designed for modular application in public spaces: betting shops, train stations, amusement arcades, nightclubs, and shopping centers. The market for the Hantarex subsequently shifted toward art galleries and museums, and the monitor has found its home in the context of the visual arts, as a much welcomed and substantial object within the ongoing process of dematerialization on the level of the art object. With its sleek and minimal design, most commonly consisting of a black straight-edged cube with no visible buttons—at least from the front—the Hantarex monitor became a specialist exhibition object. In addition, Hantarex monitors were something of an oddity in the 1980s and 1990s, since their pricing prevented them from becoming household objects, so they were effectively only accessible to citizens in the context of art exhibitions. This rarity also enabled and still enables artists and institutions to distinguish between more consumerist and domestic—entertaining—modes of engaging with the TV medium, and their "own" artistic venues and categories for channeling video art content, connoted by the Hantarex monitor's distinct and separated display characteristics.

It is puzzling that we have come to think of the Hantarex monitor as a blank, interchangeable vessel for the purposes of channeling content only. Considering its objecthood, one cannot ignore its design history, highly

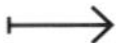

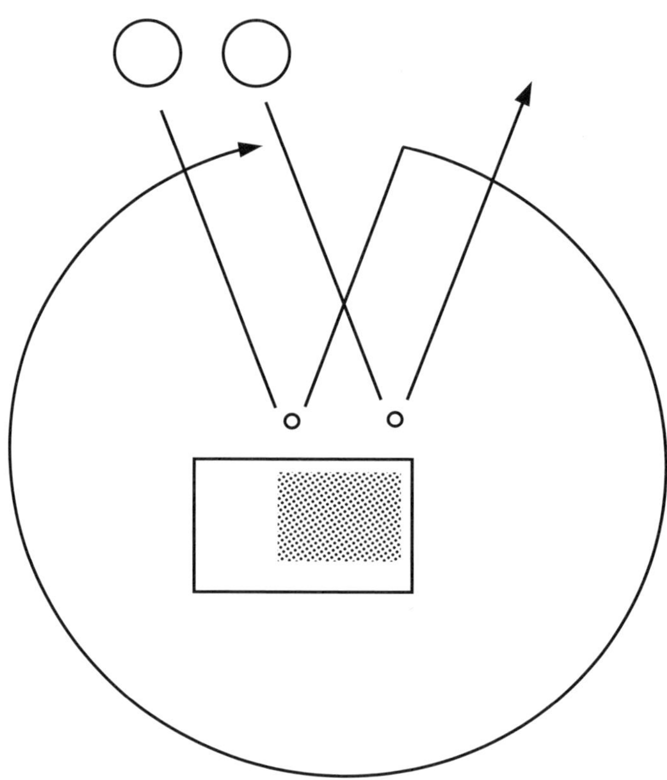

Choreography for two visitors and one monitor with a single headphone channel specific technological capacity, subcultural aesthetic, social context, and its relationship to the human body. Speaking in a thick, sweaty voice, the Hantarex has a strong sense of inherent grounding, a poignant earthly character, with an inclination to point and tilt downward. With its monolithic appearance and the average weight of a teenager, the body of a Hantarex could be considered a key player in counterbalancing the seemingly ephemeral, sometimes liminal parameters of an exhibition space, along with the immaterial nature of the video file. It goes without saying that the widespread interest in the Hantarex monitor by artists and exhibition-makers alike is often based on its rapid obsolescence paired with its formal qualities, which effectively evokes a type of potent and viable nostalgia. However, amid the legacy of the registration and documentation of the body in Hantarex-era video art, it seems important to underscore that the monitor could also be appreciated for its organic, physical, and almost fleshy existence. When mounted on a stand or suspended from a ceiling by means of strong steel wires, the body of the monitor is given limbs. The self-supporting body of the Hantarex is lifted to correspond to the scale of the human body, supporting the visitor's desire for optimized viewing conditions, and, simultaneously, positing the two players' bodies on the same level, grounding and balancing each other.

1 This model still had rounded edges, unlike the square model we have come to know today.

2 "Hantarex S.p.A. was taken over by Sambers Italia S.p.A. in 1996. Sambers Italia had already produced its first Hantarex MGG monitor in 1989, and was active as a company from 1965 within the field of professional electronic video, a business that has largely been intertwined with the world of information and communications specifically intended for public places. The MGG became known and well regarded for the spectacularization of image display." "Hantarex EQ/3 28," *The Block*, accessed August 1, 2016, http://www.the-block.org/equipment/hantarex-eq3-28%E2%80%B3/.

NORMAN DOOR

It had been deliberated at length whether the set of doors, envisioned as a replacement for the ones leading from the foyer to the main exhibition hall, could be written off as an expense. The two current and adjacent doors were designed in the late 1980s as an integral feature of the original architectural design, by an architect who was not necessarily part of the Memphis Group, but had freely borrowed the style of Ettore Sottsass' "Beverly Cabinet." With its clashing hues of yellow and green, along with its snakeskin print, the doors had always proved to be an obstacle. One door was immovable, but retained an impression of a certain motility, whereas the other door—the one with a handle—would invariably strike the other because it was used as a push-into-the-space door, when in fact it was intended for a pull-and-reveal-yourself motion.

Under the auspices of (Donald Arthur) Norman, a staff meeting was convened in order to conclusively face this reversed logic. Conservationist measures were proposed: to provide each door with "fixed" and "pull" labels. This was contested by the majority of staff members as it would contravene the initial mission statement and the "experiential discovery" ideals of the institution, whose building was also on the verge of acquiring the heritage label of an "outstanding example of the heyday of postmodern architecture." Others claimed that, in times of new institutional sincerity, there was a change needed, and that, in accordance with Norman's views of design, a set of more human-centered doors should be implemented. Here it was argued that the institution—as a space predominantly frequented by humans—should cater to human cognitive behaviors and thought patterns by prioritizing the visitors' experience and optimizing viewing conditions even further. Additionally, it was noted that certain visitors had given the institution low ratings on TripAdvisor, with one comment reading: "Because of their stubborn nature, the doors did not open promptly at 10 a.m."

A third commentary was provided by an assistant curator who recalled an article about a doorstop that had ceased to perform its task. The article claimed that what is considered broken or no longer present should be thought of as an indication of the object's vocation, its willpower, and its ability to act. Rather than a flaw, its "brokenness" underscores our mutual dependency in being with and next to things, and it in fact increases the objects agency as a non-human actant. Paraphrasing another text, the assistant promptly proclaimed: "Walls are a nice invention, but if there were no holes in them, there would be no way to get in or out; they would be mausoleums or tombs. The problem is that, if you make holes in the walls, anything and anyone can get in and out (bears, visitors, dust, rats, noise). So architects invented this hybrid: a hole-wall, often called a door, which, although common enough, has always struck me as a miracle of technology."[1] Concluding, the assistant then proposed to further examine the problematic of heritage conservation and contextualization versus present-day functionality and pragmatism regarding objects—essentially prompted by this set of doors—by hosting a symposium to sort the matter out.

While the staff discussion faltered slightly after this proclamation, it was soon met by a suggestion to place the doors on display next to their original location, a proposition that would pragmatically solve the issue at hand, and simultaneously honor the intricate design and objecthood of the two doors. This measure was unanimously agreed upon.

1   Jim Johnson and Bruno Latour, "Mixing Humans with Non-Humans: Sociology of a Door-Closer," *Social Problems* 35, no. 3 (June 1988): 298–310.

ODRADEK

One's first impression of it is of a flat, star-shaped reel of thread, and indeed it appears to have thread entwined in it; admittedly only broken old pieces of thread, in all sorts of colours and thicknesses, knotted or even tangled together. But it's not a reel, since a little rod emerges from the centre of the star, and this rod has another rod going off it at right angles. With this rod on one side, and one of the points of the star on the other, the whole thing is able to stand upright as on two feet.[1]

Remember Franz Kafka's story "The Worries of a Head of Household"? The text revolves around the Odradek, a peculiar, physical, and indefinable living object that "stays alternately in the attic, on the staircase, in the corridors, and in the hall."[2] The Odradek has no fixed abode; it shifts from location to location, not to be seen for months, but always returning to the house of its owner, the family man. The Odradek is a metaphysical rupture in the reality of the family man, one that makes him aware of the fact that the object will most likely outlive him—and the story equally provides an epistemological rupture in the reality of the reader. The story of the Odradek, like the figure itself, is a paradox: to realize that the Odradek stands as an antithesis to meaning and interpretation is to have already infused it with meaning, wrapped in language by the reader. Once this final interpretation is made, the text of the Odradek and its impossible formation through meaning and interpretation should dissolve in your hands, but it does not, and the discourse continues…

The Odradek may be asked questions, but it will answer in an abstract manner.

1 Franz Kafka, "The Worries of a Head of Household," in *Metamorphosis and Other Stories*, trans. Michael Hofmann (London: Penguin Books, 2007), 211.

2 Walter Benjamin, "Franz Kafka. On the Tenth Anniversary of His Death" [1931], in *Illuminations*, trans. Harry Zorn (London: Pimlico, 1999), 129.

OPENING

The moments prior to the exhibition opening are imbued with great anticipation and paranoid readings of undesired factors that might be noticed—factors that eventually will only be known to those actively engaged in the process leading up to the exhibition. A final turn and a straightening, a consideration of the right angle, obscuring and hiding anomalies with duct tape, a final touch of filler and paint, randomly stacking those objects and tools that proved helpful and then became undesired on top of each other in the storage space, cleaning dirty glasses, and waiting for the drinks delivery. This preparatory window is a set of cliché acts of self-censorship that are repeatedly and unmistakably reaffirmed.

Upon its disclosure to an imagined but yet to be determined public, the exhibition at its moment of opening is positioned to mark a rupture in the durational existence to which the space is aligned. The space gradually fills itself with bodies and their voices of differing natures, volumes, and tones—among which we hear opinions, comments, gossip, and hearsay. Connections between and with the objects are actively vocalized and implied within the undulating movement of clusters of objects and entities being bound and unbound. A fascinating self-celebratory pulsation rhythm is going on—"What project are you working on?"—the intensity of which may lead a brave institutional body to postpone their future opening receptions with their seeming negligence of object-beings, to instead host the opening midway, or to go against the market mechanism of climax-after-climax and avoid the opening altogether.

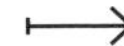

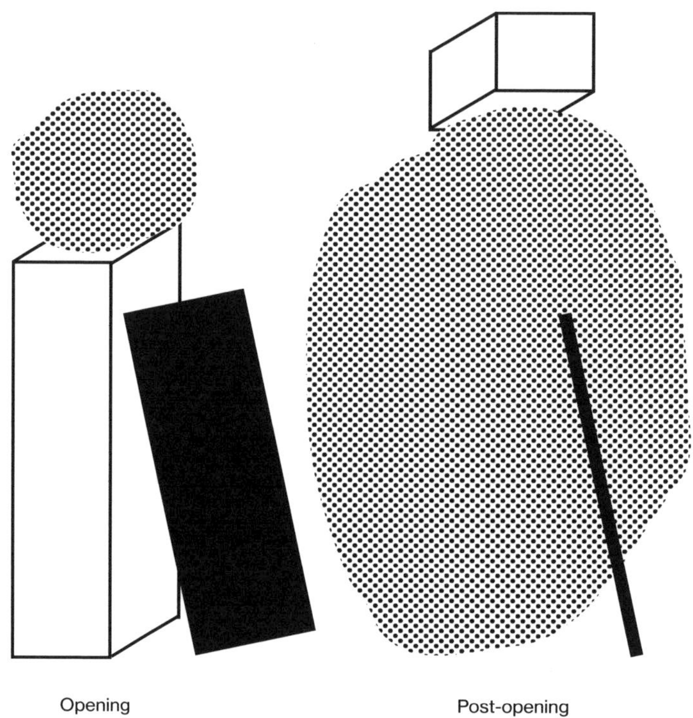

Opening
Post-opening

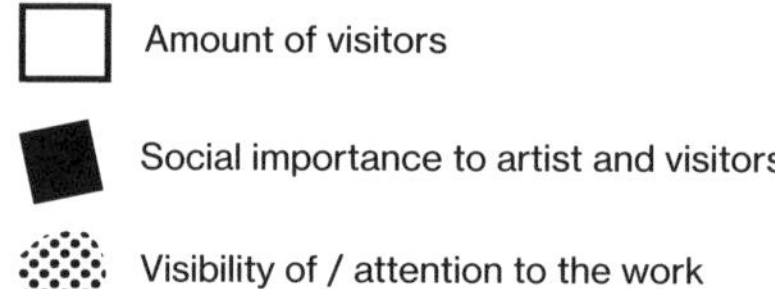

Amount of visitors
Social importance to artist and visitors
Visibility of / attention to the work

To introduce oxygen as the sovereign object to which most, if not all, objects and entities conform and adhere, seems to be beyond the point. To think of oxygen as the ultimate ground of access, and, in the case of this text, as the principal prerequisite for (human) beings to access and encounter, perceive and process an exhibition, we could also consider oxygen as a prerequisite for institutional subsistence. Here it proves helpful to assert the interdependence between the formation of oxygen and its replenishment from the photosynthesis of organisms, among them plants and trees, which are, in turn, dependent on sunlight and water. The all-encompassing notion of oxygen as the principle to all thinkable principles is partially overcome in this light, as it is equally bound to and dependent on a system of constantly exchanged interrelations.

On the level of respiration, however, we might as well attribute to oxygen the role of outlining the possibilities for thinking, in the sense that oxygen could be considered as the kind of massively distributed "hyper-object"—a term coined by philosopher Timothy Morton—that is phased and nonlocal to such an extent that it transcends the possibility of human perception, and is thus also able to bypass thought.[1] Its given-ness is beyond our grasp. Because the notion that humans are interconnected with oxygen is often readily agreed upon as something evident in advance, as a solid ground from which other, less fundamental and essentialist thought processes can be induced, oxygen is mostly abandoned as an active figure of thought.

To make oxygen the object of interrogation in the context of an exhibition might seem far-fetched, but what is to be said about hosting an exhibition in the absence of oxygen? Would we be able to truly grapple with oxygen as a subject, topic, and thematic as exemplified by several recorded and staged instances of the absence of oxygen, in the shape of documentation, or would we only gain a sense of our interconnectedness with oxygen, as an object that is perpetually active, if we could somehow become physically aware of its absence? Critical institutional and off-grid zones in the shape of containers devoid of oxygen molecules could be provided—like

underwater, extraterrestrial, and other oxygen vacuums—to function as hosts for exhibitions that exceed the present zones of display comfort, and act as active and additional layers in the rethinking of the interrelations and interconnectedness between objects.

1   Timothy Morton, *Hyperobjects: Philosophy and Ecology After the End of the World* (Minnesota: University of Minnesota Press, 2013).

PEDESTAL

A pedestal is not that different from a plinth, or any kind of base for that matter.[1]

1 To believe a Google image search (shun the nonbeliever), pedestals are ornate structures, approximating a smaller version of the classical column, whereas plinths are more rigid and angular. The pedestal is brought into existence to negotiate between a structure and the ground, and, in paraphrasing the words of Scott Burton, is "a specialized form of table."[1] As a levitation device, the pedestal is rooted in a longstanding and persistent anthropological lineage, one in which the objects hosted by the pedestal are refused physical contact with the ground, and are thought of in terms of being removed and altered from the time and functionality of "objects in general." The thing about a pedestal is that when you are using it, you are not looking at the pedestal itself. Could a sculpture of a pedestal also function as pedestal beyond the representational regime, and, more specifically, could a pedestal have a dual identity, be doubled? Could it be two or more things simultaneously?

However, our engagements with the pedestal are only durational in nature, insofar as pedestals are formalized and rationalized as mere placeholders: they are there to negate close proximity and physical contact, and to enforce a spatial and psychological distance in order to allow for a particular kind of dedicated perceptual foregrounding. Consequently, many objects have descended from the pedestal into the "real" and "lived" space of the viewer, or the pedestal-object and the cohabiting object have proposed to merge and coalesce: disintegrating and dissolving values and inequalities around support and lead, shadow and spotlight.[2]

1 Oscar Tuazon, "Scott Burton," Giuliani Foundation Website, accessed July 18, 2016, http://www.fondazionegiuliani.org/category/exhibitions/scott-burton-en/?lang=en.

2 An interesting continuation of this discussion is provided in: Manuela Ammer, "Das Sockelproblem," *frieze d/e* (Autumn 2011): 60–9.

<table>
<tr><td>(50)</td></tr>
<tr><td>**PEDESTAL II**</td></tr>
</table>

Put me on a pedestal and I will only disappoint you.
—Courtney Barnett

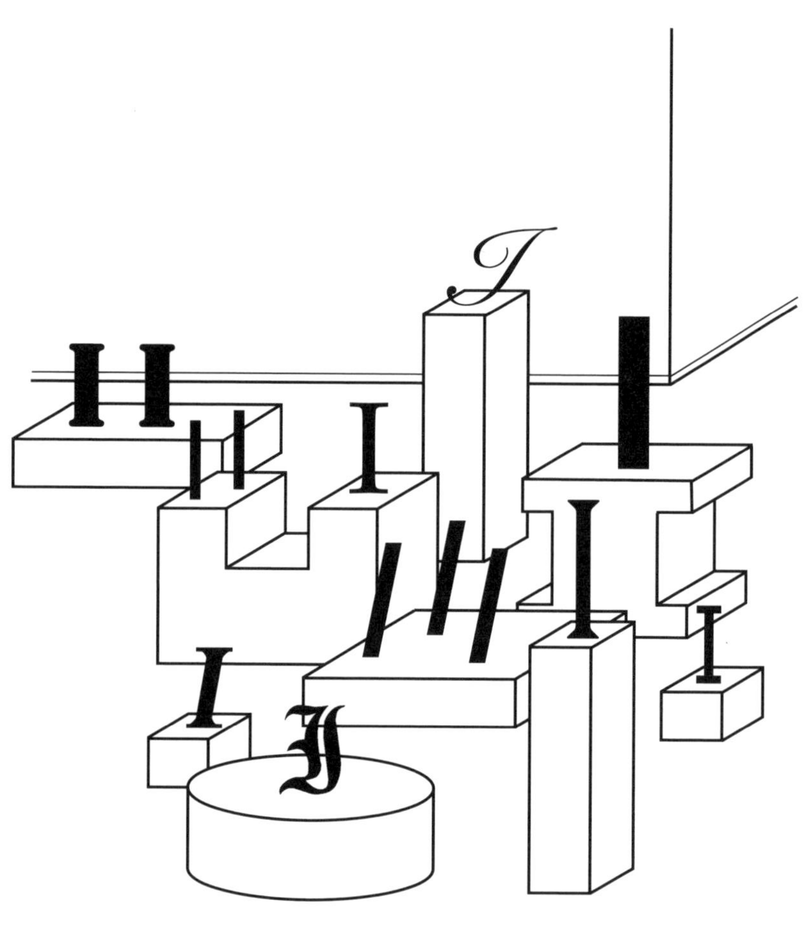

(51)

PLANTS

Sometime around September 2012, in the concrete jungle of London, I found myself surrounded by various types of exotic and tropical plants, among them palm trees, banana plants, and a mini-palm from Hawaii. The Hawaiian mini-palm is an interesting species: it maintains its native and innate growing cycle, characterized by the shedding of its yellow leaves during the European spring and summer (or rather the plant's autumn and winter).

An increasing proliferation of plant arrangements in both domestic spaces and exhibition contexts indicates what we might perhaps call, using the words of Dominique Gonzalez-Foerster, a certain "tropicalization of the mind": an increased interest in an approximation of the vegetal other within the stable and protected confines of the domestic human environment.[1] Tacitly posited in the background, somewhere between living and inert, the plant serves as an emblem of mental tranquility, plentitude, and stability—whereas the ecological mutations of the Anthropocene continue to thrive elsewhere, out of lateral sight. Indoor plant cultivation could be understood as a way of not taking up the troubling task of *regrounding* and finding ways of living in capitalist ruins, and rearranging the Titanic's deck chairs instead.

Indeed, the present cultivation of house plants seems to exemplify vegetal passion as a lifestyle attribute, perhaps serving as a reference to tamed, neutralized nature—the type of nature that is always located elsewhere and over there, functioning as a seemingly stable backdrop for human activity. This is a somewhat naïve, neo-hippy retro-vision of humankind and its surrounding natural environs rejoicing in warm earth music for plants and the people who love them.[2]

In the frame of exhibition making we can equally discern a shift in the deployment of the plant, moving from accessory to artistic device. In the period between 1860 and 1980, with its heyday in the 1960s and 1970s, plants "naturally" punctuated art exhibitions, as collateral elements of an

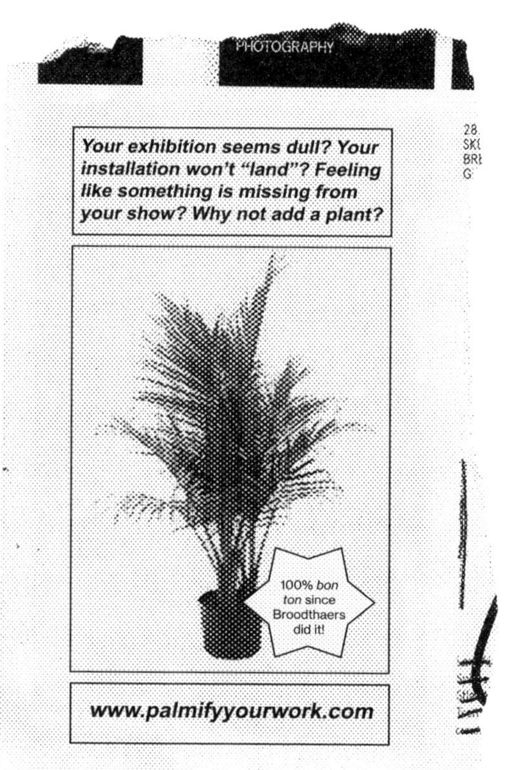

PHOTOGRAPHY

Your exhibition seems dull? Your installation won't "land"? Feeling like something is missing from your show? Why not add a plant?

100% *bon ton* since Broodthaers did it!

www.palmifyyourwork.com

institutional style, perhaps equal to chairs and tables. Functionally speaking, plants also served as decorative natural screens and vegetal walls, positioned to hide fire extinguishers, or to keep visitors from entering certain exhibition areas. Next to the subcategory of "exhibition plants," we could name those works of art that involve and revolve around plants, starting from Marcel Broodthaers, as a notable advocate of the palm tree as a figure of speech, to John Baldessari and his aim to teach a plant the alphabet, as more classical examples of plant-being as art subject.

At the moment of writing, art galleries and institutional spaces are replete with plants, but now more often as an integral part of an art object or installation—an observation often made by frequent visitors of contemporary art exhibitions. However, moving away from stylization and the activation of the plant for its graphic qualities, its formal values, and decorative function, what lies behind this plant increase is a more significant and engaging context: that of "plant-thinking," a type of "thinking without the head" that stimulates affective and non-cognitive dialogue with our surroundings—allowing us, humankind, to think and propose new modes of reception, sensuous thinking, and tacit sensitivity.[3]

How then to approach the kinship between a plastic plant and a rubber plant?

1   The phrase "tropicalization of the mind" was cited by Dominique Gonzalez-Foerster in "New Beauty" (artist talk, hosted by De Appel arts centre, Stadsschouwburg, Amsterdam, June 22, 2009).

2   The 1970s saw a strong increase in the release of vinyl records for plants *and* humans. Here one could think of album titles like: *Flowering Conversations: Talking to Your Plants* (Ken Nordine and Alice A. McNally, 1969); *Music to Grow Plants* (Dr. George Milstein, 1970); *Plants Are Like People* (Jerry Baker, 1973); *Green Sounds (Music for Your Plants)* (Steve Hall, 1974); *A Chant for Your Plants* (Ann Chase, 1976); *Mother Earth's Plantasia* (Mort Garson, 1976); *Plant Talk/Sound Advice* (Roth and Bricker, 1976); and *De La Musique Et Des Secrets Pour Enchanter Vos Plantes* (Roger Roger and Martin Monestier, 1978).

3   This argument is paraphrased from: Michael Marder, *Plant-Thinking: A Philosophy of Vegetal Life* (New York: Columbia University Press, 2013).

PLINTH-BEING

Here you are, time and again, both unnoticed and historicized before our eyes. Kept alive at times when resources were scarce and you proved durable. Embraced, even, by Bruce McLean in 1971, although it was a short affair at best.[1] An initial flirtation with your boldness turned into an uncomfortable and stiff relationship. Most of all you are a poser in parts—five pieces to be exact, and more should not be necessary. You are a poser of the macho type, who works out on a daily basis, toward a square and muscular posture, and takes care of your skin more than usual, but is eventually too shy to approach anyone, let alone an imagined partner.

You blend in easily with your white surfaces, and among peers you prefer to reside in the background. Camouflage as social tactic. Your lack of anticipation, your passivity, has not gone unnoticed. In trying to show resistance, you were eventually forced to form a couple with another object, however not of your choosing. Knowing, like Marcel Duchamp perhaps did, that your freedom could only be acquired by using the currency of the regime that governs you, you seek your inscription in the firmament by speaking a hyper-formalist language, imposed with a high degree of self-awareness.

Ever since you succeeded in establishing partnerships, you entered into many relations: couplings that only lasted between one and three months. During these short periods of great intensity, your inherent properties and qualities came to the fore, and, in recalling Martin Heidegger's ideas on the notion of *Gestell*, you excelled at framing your partners, at being a standing reserve, supporting them all to exist in the world, to be seen and understood.

1   This is a reference to Bruce McLean's work *Pose Work for Plinths 3* (1971). Other examples in which plinths serve as the subject (matter) of an artwork and become art objects in their own right include: Piero Manzoni's *Base of the World* (1961); Robert Morris' *Untitled (Mirrored Cubes)* (1966); Sol LeWitt's *Serial Project I (ABCD)* (1966); Larry Bell's *20" Untitled 1969 (Tom Messer Cube)* (1969); Donald Judd's *Untitled (Six Boxes)* (1974); Tom Friedman's *Untitled (A Curse)* (1992); and Ceal Floyer's *Page 11,803 of 11,083* (2010); among many current examples including works by Davide Balula, Nina Beier, Haris Epaminonda, Oliver Laric, and David Maljkovic.

PRESS RELEASE

The history of the press release is the tale of the ongoing transformation and adaptation of its potentiality. The press release as an instantly recognizable text format, a common language application of sorts ("We are proud to announce!")—at least to those who have been exposed frequently enough to its variable scales, mutations, and dialects, and have started to recognize certain stable patterns through experience. Or even to those who perform the sentences themselves, that take part in the formation of press release texts. What about them? Their technical vocabularies, jargon, linguistic elaborations, and lofty and decadent wordings make for a sincere form of prose. The texts having often become tired of themselves.

The various incarnations and iterations of the press release are textual swamps that often reek of plagiarism—very similar, in fact, to a text revolving around the subject of the press release and its ambiguous nature. Once written, often passing through more than one writer, the press release text is set to travel through a process of far-reaching and exhilarating copyediting, and we must suspend the idea of conscious copying as no one can quite recognize the sources, or trace back to the origins of its phrases. This venture has been great so far, right? To see the extent to which a text could be stretched to reach out and measure up against the objects it set out to describe. The press release as an epistemological battleground in which linguistic structures of meaning are "forcefully" applied to structures of being, although swiftly executed as if it were a silent choreography, a painless performance. This insurmountable pile of incongruities between a language projected and an object concerned—which was perhaps neglected slightly—marks the point at which the text starts to relate more strongly to how the image looked in your head. The press release pertains to the idea of how objects arrive first and foremost in the shape of texts, as a prerequisite tool for the exhibition's mediation, its perception-making. From words on a screen to the sheet of paper in the exhibition, the press release confronts the object with the layers of texts that write it, and this amounts to a tacit and unanswered confrontation. Paradoxical perhaps, as

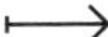

the press release is employed to accurately approach the object, to give the reader a sense of immediacy and proximity to it, while, at the same time, to be both disconnected and distant. The press release has already become something else, something in and by itself, another object employed for its referential features—a page covered in language.

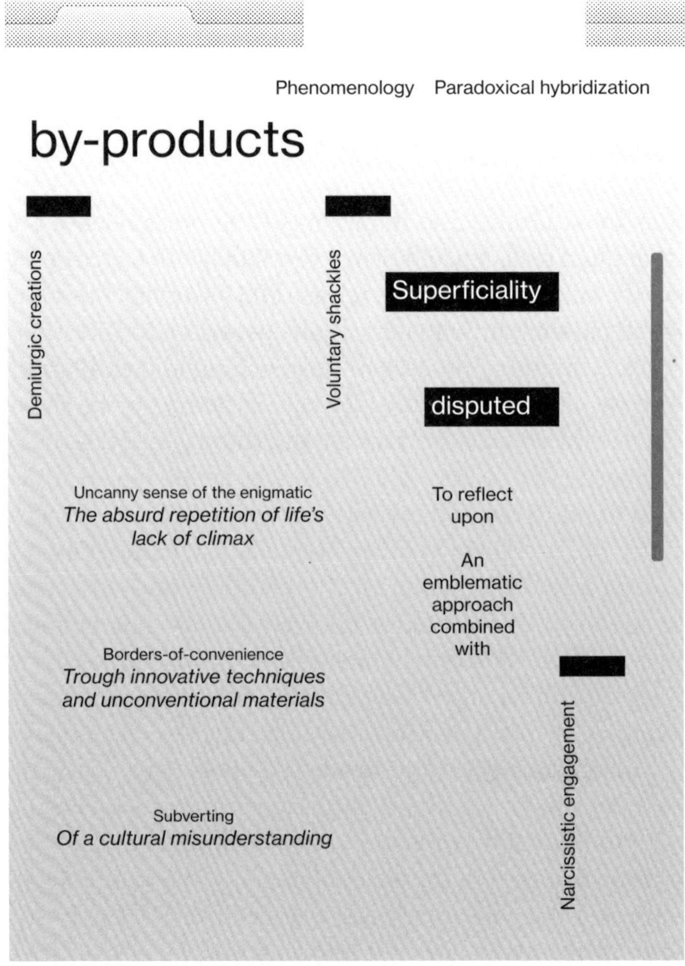

**PROJECTION
BOOTH**

From the brightly lit exhibition space we are drawn into a narrow corridor, and a sharp turn after about 3 meters points toward a pitch-black room. Along the way, at the corner, the walls begin to be clad with gray egg-carton-like foam. I call out to my friend, who is just behind me, but the only thing I hear is the hollow and muffled sound of my own voice.

The projection booth is a tactile obstacle insofar as it defies any spectatorship until a certain familiarization with the space concerned is achieved. Upon the gradual perceptual disclosure of what seems to be the projection booth and its small constructed entrance path, there is an instance of light flickering at the end of the corridor—triggering a curiosity for something that is yet to be discovered. To set forth into a projection booth is to willingly suspend one's point of view and to rely on one's sense of touch. Groping, for example, becomes a key skill, as visitors will tend to fixate on what their eyes have adjusted to, but will eventually end up stumbling over the viewing bench that remained invisible.

Having landed on the bench slightly unfortunately, and while reflecting on your uncoordinated behavior, your aching knee, and the other spatial deceptions you might have managed to avoid, some hints of light will settle on your retina, revealing that you have not spent these painstakingly long minutes by yourself, and that three people were in fact leaning against the back wall. Only later does the third person turn out to be an oversized backpack. You begin to notice the respectively limited size of the space that is somewhat closing in on itself, and the accompanying sound of an overly dominant projector that distracts you to the point at which you surrender to the hammering rhythm of its rattling utterances.

Ultimately, the projection booth is a persistent and demanding object that exposes its entrails to the process of unwillingly foregrounding itself in its various guises, toward a gradual mental collapse and withdrawal of its apparent nature over a diffused but highly immersive viewing experience.

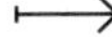

By encapsulating and absorbing its subjects, who slowly attune and render themselves sensitive to their new temporal habitat, the projection booth posits a suspended sense of viewership, evidenced in the subject's loss of bodily control and an acute awareness of being suspended within an estranging environment. The subject's loss is later recovered in their morphing from a floating, suspended body into a viewing body directed toward a projective surface. Here the booth gives rise to a different type of transformation, from projected material on screen to another potential transposal and displacement of the body to a non-discrete set of locations, places, ideas, and fictions. Indeed, where the projection booth ends and the work begins.

(55)

PROJECTION SCREEN (FLOATING)

Imagine a screenplay. Not one that takes place on the screen in the shape of projected images, or one performed in the smoky area between projector and screen so often evoked in Nouvelle Vague films, but a reversed, somewhat introspective play that leads us back to the projection screen performing itself on stage. For this entry is concerned with the floating projection screen: a surface suspended in the air, an object that is dependent on the support of supposedly transparent (yet ultimately visible) wires and hooks to materialize its capabilities as a hovering entity. These prosthetics are key, as they aid in the screen's detachment from both floor and wall, and act in cooperation with it.

In being secured and lifted at different points, there is a semblance of genuine levitation, and I suppose the screen is really floating, but the suggestive element hinges on the appearance of the screen's independence — hence the employment of transparent wire. The illusion of this appearance could as well be thought of as the prioritization of the interplay between the screen and its respective space within the exhibition: the screen folds the space by providing another plane, and the twisted degree of its placement makes the space move at an angle. We are witness to a screenplay of detachments from the given architectural parameters through which the screen propels itself into space. A spatial shape-shifting that also partially negotiates the extent to which other objects are scaled, made more or less visible, detached or withdrawn; the screen recreates the space of the exhibition by instigating newly formed passageways and walking routes, casting shadows and creating silent choreographies.

<table>
<tr><td>(56)

PUBLIC</td><td>Built on the solid foundations of the republic, the public for an exhibition is best defined as a demographic phantom of the institution. Both fleeting and unstable, the envisioned public is constantly becoming, but never quite arriving. In an attempt to mark its pres-</td></tr>
</table>

ence, and for its external environs to be brought in, the exhibition is likely to have a potential and envisioned public, one that is ungraspable and yet to be determined, one that has to be invented and reached out for.

From the perspective of the exhibition's initiators, this envisioned public might then be based upon and constituted by projections of a quantified and proliferating multiplication of like-minded spirits (the peer-to-peer network). Or, rather, from the perspective of the communications department, one might think of abstract, imagined, undefined, and amalgamated figures and categories that come to represent the public: a blob-like *apeiron* now suddenly consisting of and fragmenting into various malleable target groups (youth, intellectuals, urban professionals, culture lite users, etc.). Here, labels are attached and categories are established to demarcate the outlines of people "out there," which, by their very nature, are fragmented, dispersed, and differentiated, but are shaped into coherent wholes by the communications department, for the sake of brevity and a mutual understanding among colleagues.

In order to solidify this public body as an envisioned potential, a measuring scale is a helpful tool. Take the Facebook event as an example: the intention to become an active member of an exhibition's public often proves to be an empty promise, informed by a general overdose of events (time pressure meets high performance vs. the fear of missing out). Social platforms generally lack the capacity—and often only succeed partially—to actively enhance, activate, and mobilize those members of the public that constitute the social fabric needed to activate an exhibition. Perhaps similar to extending invitations to birthday parties and housewarmings, the reliance on a peer-to-peer exhibition public is a promising starting point, but bear in mind that at least 50 percent of attendees will be staying at home.

SHELF

Whereas it could be asserted that both the plinth and the pedestal are common to the interior grammar of the exhibition, the shelf, by comparison, is a more ambiguous device—one that hovers above the heavy grounding of its aforementioned peers. The shelf could be considered as a part of exhibition vernacular that only appears on special occasions, acting along, but preferring to return home and resonate in its natural habitat: its commonly implied domestic setting.

However, this attitude is not a matter of principle. On public outings of the exhibitionist kind, perhaps quite unexpectedly, the shelf successfully negotiates a whole set of different relations with itself, its neighbors, and its surroundings. Compared to its family members that tend toward providing a stage for single and autonomous performances and object lessons, the shelf prefers to rejoice in the collective and inclusive spirit of the conga line of flat ontology: "and you, and you, and you…" (and not only my ontology).

It could be said that the life of the shelf is limited because of its interdependence with and necessary alignment to the temporal and spatial characteristics of the wall and the space that host its surface. Here, the shelf object is endangered from at least two angles that mathematically denote the dimensions of its shape, its beginning, and its end—although it refuses to think in that order. Having retreated, now designated as a mere fixture, the shelf decides to hold on tight, knowing that it is, in fact, hosting the party.

<table>
<tr><td>(58)

SKYPING</td><td>The Skype notification has been sounding for some time, while I was finishing a cigarette. I do not want to be seen "smoking on Skype," and odd as it may seem, second-to-third-hand smoke may actually apply here. For me at least. I am greeting you on my</td></tr>
</table>

tablet display. You are still in Brazil, smoking a cigarette, and getting ready to fly to London in three days. On the surface, you look slightly more distorted and greenish than last time we Skyped, but that might well be the video quality.

After some awkward talking (about projects) and nervous laughter (about other, less successful projects), I propose to walk you through the exhibition space and update you on the progress made on the installation of your work. I hope you do not have smoke in your eyes. I am single-handedly navigating your vision right now. Knowing that all spatial dimensions collapse on screen, which only gives a 22.7 by 32.5 centimeter impression of the space and a hint of perspective by successive shapes, scales, and color intensities, I am trying to make your perception less blurred and pixelated through description, and by talking about the team's decision-making thus far.

Our tour comes to an abrupt end. The bandwidth could not support the time difference any longer, and, unknowingly, for the last three minutes, I was having a monologue while your feed fractured and collapsed into segments of uneven intensity.

I look for the Skype chat option.

"Let's take it from here."
"I will send you an e-mail."

Skype stems from Estonia.

Skype makes it "simple to share experiences with the people that matter to you, wherever they are."

"I hope you don't have smoke in your eyes."

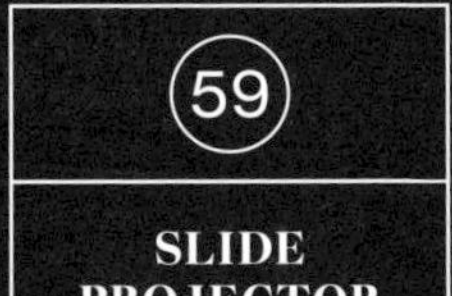

[Performed model: KODAK Ektapro 7000]
[Accompanied by a constant buzzing]

TIC

CLICK
CLACK

CLICK CLACK, CLICK CLACK, CLICK CLACK

PRRRRRRRRRRRRRRRRRRRRRRRRRRRRRRRRRRRRR
RRRRRRRRRRRRRRRRRRRRRRRRRRRRRRRRRRRRRR
RRRRRRRRRRRRRRRRRRRRRR

[8 . 3 3   s e c o n d s]

[R o t a t e   3 6 0   d e g r e e s]

It is not called a wheel, it is called a carousel.
And we will move forward from here...

Hit the button. No, the dial. The dial on the remote. The remote dial.

Moving forward, moving forward, moving forward,
moving forward, moving forward
Click clack, click clack, click clack, click clack, click clack

AND hit reverse!

CLICK CLACK

I am going to focus it a little with the zoom lens feature.
Special feature.

Focus, focus focus, focus, focus focus, focus,
FOCUSSSSZZZZZZZZZZZZZZZZ
ZZZZZ, ZZZZZ-HMMMM, ZZZZZ, ZZZZZ-HMMMM,
ZZZZZ, ZZZZZ-ZZZZZ-HMMMM

CLICK CLACK

TRRRRRRRRRRRRRRRRRRRRRRRRRRRRRRRRR

Looks like a jam.

[U n t i l   t h e   s l i d e   i s   r e m o v e d]   T I C

SOCKET

Extending beyond the practicalities of the impending power bill, the electricity socket forms a pivotal part in the supply chain of currency and exchange. The socket is the pleasant interlocutor between external forces and indoor activities, a midpoint that enables a complex network of relations, among them art objects relying on its distributed output. However, as one of the often readily present and scattered elements in the interior grammar of the exhibition space, the electricity socket cannot be considered a secondary object, or merely an element of architecture. That is to say, the socket has a currency of its own. A currency that extends well beyond the contrived anthropomorphic qualities of its electric pin holes that mimic some key features present in the human face—especially explicit in the Danish-type plug socket. Equally, the idea of a socket coming alive and acting in the space as a ghost of previous architectural states and functions is deceitful. A seemingly solitary socket on an empty wall, suspended in the air, might indeed prove to be a deception of sorts, but this animation of the socket as a being should not lead us to the flow of energy disappearing from this object when it presents itself to us. The electricity socket quite clearly determines and negotiates a substantial part of the internal trafficking and routing of power through the exhibition space. Not as a means to an end, but rather as an inherent quality that is acting as part of a largely obscured world of objects exercising their power in a networked relation. Here the distinctions between what is acting and what is being acted upon start to dissolve, and, instead of jumping to a conclusion about the differences between supplier and receiver, we are called to think of a congruent whole that accommodates both.

SOUND SHOWER

In great anticipation of your vocalized presence, and as we are undoubtedly honored to have you, we have devised a dedicated aural space in which you can freely reign, one that takes into account both your noisiness and our auditory wellbeing. An apparatus, a device of our making, resembling an inverted saucer with a sound emitting cone, that steers sound waves in such a directional manner that it will mark your territory with an immaculate audio footprint. Call it an auditory hotspot if you will. One that will leave competing institutions wanting one of their own.

The sound shower—as common language has come to call the apparatus—leaves no room for any kind of leakage, or for the spillage of any valuable content. It is tailored to enclose every sample, every droplet of perceptible audio material. As viewed from a distance, the sound shower is an invaluable device in facilitating a diplomatic truce within a polyphonic assemblage. Not necessarily as a way to join them all together, but, rather, in respect of their varying constitutions, we find ourselves making a call in which some overly present actors are isolated. Not always willingly, but at least everyone is being heard.

This audibility on the level of the exhibition as assembly, as common ground, seems to be based on democratic principles insofar as the selected majority of noisemakers preside over the minority of mutes. During the preparation of an exhibition, opinions and judgments are exchanged in regard to who speaks the loudest and with the most substantial reach (and will most likely account for the greatest number of supporters, in populist thinking at least), and who speaks the most eloquently and intimately (and therefore may require a dedicated stage). Remember, these laws are by no means given, but rather are made between spokespeople representing the members of the group.

Reaching the point at which the majority is silenced—although this majority consists of already silent onlookers and inhabitants engaged in other activities—the remainder of the speaking subjects are placed in separate,

dedicated zones, silenced by means of headphones, placed in a sound shower, or relocated to another room with ample insulation.

To further the sonic balance of an exhibition, one must adjust and sometimes, rather unfortunately, one may lose part of one's acoustic identity in the process, you do understand? Do you?

SPIRIT LEVEL

The thin straight line of mathematical reason must not be crossed, although it remains to be seen whether the logic of the horizontal and vertical, both imposed and imparted, should be questioned, undone, and performed differently. For what reason? Why challenge the notion that reality strictly corresponds to the total sum of sensed phenomena, especially if the phenomena are measured by another kind of agent in the form of a spirit or laser? The human eye and its lateral perspective can be extended and calibrated by placing another tool-being between the body and the to-be-sensed phenomenon, in order to overcome unperceivable visual distortions and incongruities. These tool-beings are constructed and programmed in such a way that they correspond with our views and expectations of the objectively straight, the horizontal, and the linear: the perfect register for affirming a known, given, and consciously apprehended reality. They come to our aid, perform our registry of expectations, and, after checking if our desires remain the same and that the demands are practically possible, we adjust our situation accordingly (the alignment, the projection, and so forth). Behave straightly! It's my desire! It's my desire! Is it? Did you know the floor is not straight and is actually rather jolly? So things are a bit askew. The retinal tool-being is currently unable to perform a straight sentence. Did you know the wall is not straight and is actually rather warped? So things are a bit askew.

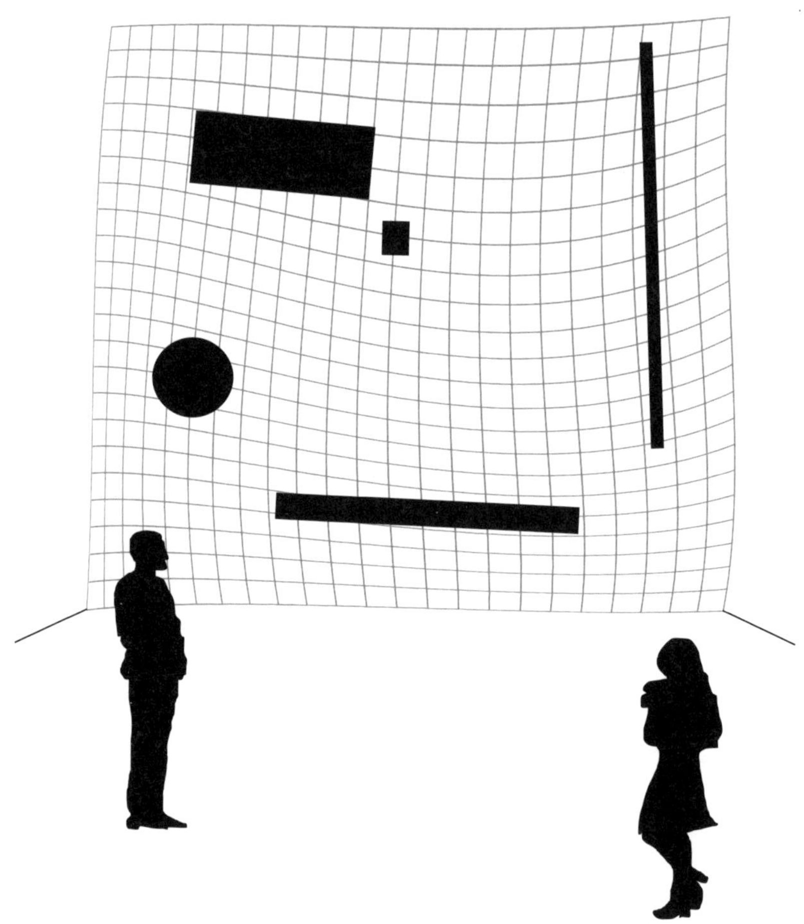

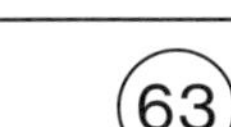

SPOTLIGHT

What does it mean to face desire so reluctantly? To welcome your guests, to host them within the safe and warm limits of your spectral appearance, to be reminded time and again that someone turned you on, and then someone turned on you. Here, indeed, we find the spotlight to be among the most generous and serving of actants commonly present in an exhibition. A resident and abiding subject that will stay in place, even if the guests have decided to leave early. Although the spotlight issues gentle whispering invitations that it would never direct toward itself, it might nurture a desire to be seen, to become its own protagonist on an epic journey of conflict and reconciliation with other light sources. There might be a performance at night, when the spotlights shine like stars. Dim the lights, you can guess the rest…

STORAGE

With no collection to house, the institution's storage instead accumulated items considered to be either useful or valuable, often shrouded in Bubble Wrap, cardboard boxes, or crates. Soon enough, this exterior packaging started to supersede the actual items contained, leaving only the exaggerated material contours and the occasional label affixed to its exterior in order to assist the eventual recognition of the object contained. Passing their time on racks in rooms, these storage occupants often remain in a dormant state for extended periods of standby and readiness, until they are recalled to go on show. Instead of attaining an ongoing afterlife in storage, most of the inhabitants exchange their gradual acclimatization for more lively and different roles elsewhere.

The storage, however, is undoubtedly left as a site of ongoing accumulation, no matter how many itinerant or seemingly permanent residents may uphold their truthful claims to permanent inhabitation. Here, the storage has effectively become invaluable to the institution's adaptive qualities. In order to uphold the organic continuum of the institution's internal flows, the storage functions as an accumulative organ presiding over short-term memories and exhibition leftovers, a repository and register of previous states. To maintain a healthy balance, and to prevent the storage from clogging, a set of dietary checks and balances will have to be carried out regularly: What to discard, what to archive, what is capable of mutating and integrating elsewhere, on occasions to come? What may be tolerated as an integral part of one organ—the current exhibition, for instance—may equally be forcefully removed or used elsewhere. In fact, the entire facility may be ejected in an optimization effort—thrown overboard to stay lean.

To mourn the loss of storage is rather unattractive. Instead we may praise its capacity to suddenly appear elsewhere and give shelter to the temporarily abandoned, forgotten, and dismissed, those close to our hearts, yet not quite close enough.

1. Old exhibition catalogs
2. Various publications
3. Invitations for past exhibitions
4. Pedestals of various sizes
5. (Plexi)glass cases
6. Instruction manuals
7. Slide projectors
8. Media players
9. Hantarex screens
10. Power tools
11. A mess of various wires
12. Hand tools
13. Bubble Wrap
14. Various other packing materials
15. Wood
16. Interns
17. Withered plant
18. Portable bar
19. Chairs
20. A supposedly missing artwork
21. Movable wall

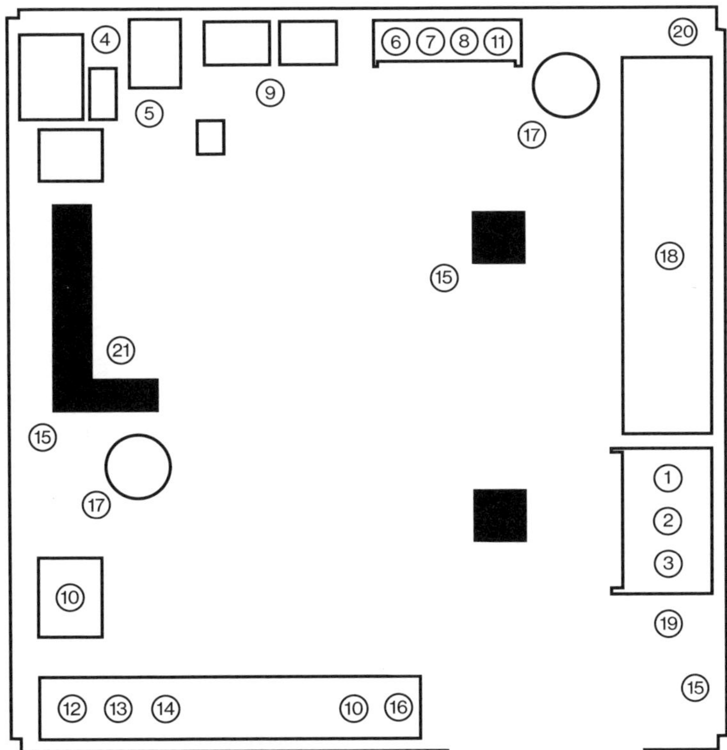

<table>
<tr><td>(65)</td></tr>
<tr><td>**TABLE AND DESK**</td></tr>
</table>

Transposed into the space of the exhibition, there are equal possibilities to exchange tables for desks, desks for tables, and so on. For instance, to inscribe a table with a labor-specific function and refer to it as a desk seems redundant inasmuch as its potential uses and functions remain expandable, detachable, and exchangeable. In fact, the wording of the previous sentence, used for common understanding, quite falsely makes both the external user and the projected function inherent to the object proper. In putting aside the table as a philosophical trope over-charged with meaning, the ping-pong-type table commonly used during installation periods—because it is foldable and storable, and simultane-ously allows for playful intervals during installation periods—could just as easily serve as a reception desk. As could the office desk serve as a communal dining table, with its drawers and bonsai. In fact, the table does not need to serve any of these purposes in order to remain thinkable as a more multidimensional entity than its seemingly fixed abode might imply.

In positing the table within the exhibition space, as a placeholder for other objects and as a temporal fixture with a shifting nature, the table could be thought of as an object that enables interactions to be framed. Here, the table serves as a place where objects land, temporarily ground them-selves, and take flight again, all the while maintaining its intrinsic qual-ities and characteristics. In short, we could consider the table as a thing that does not change and cannot be exhausted by the functions allocated to its being, by merely stapling an operating manual to its surface dictating how, and under which guise it will operate from now on.

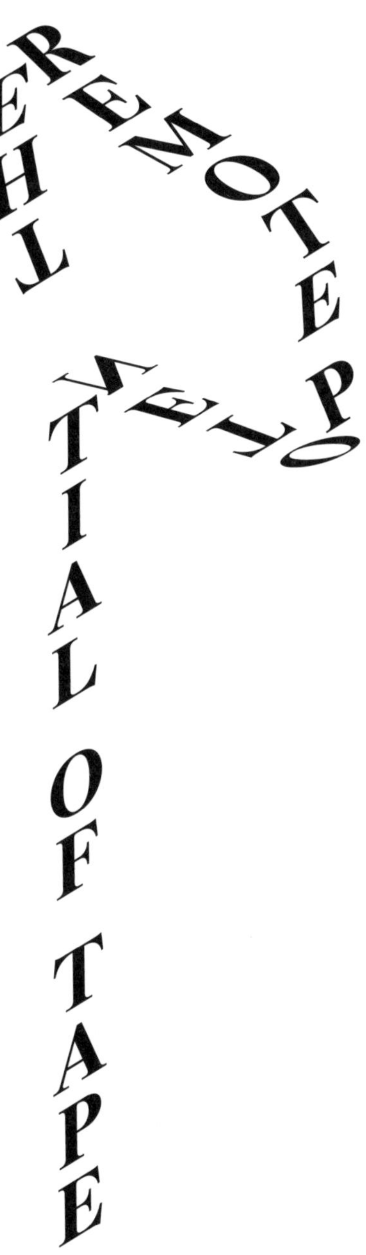

See pages:
68
84–5
92–3
144

TEMPORARILY
REMOVED
(SIGN)

I am making my way through a long shadowy corridor, lined with an almost continuous row of vitrines on my left-hand side. The row of vitrines is reminiscent of early computer-game graphics with their lack of variation: uniform, generic, and repetitive, a filler for an otherwise empty space devoid of substance, ambiance, and narrative arcs between chapters. This space, however, is very real, with dim, deep yellow light coming from the vitrines, as if the bulbs had not been cleaned following the general smoking ban in the 1990s. There is herringbone parquet throughout, and, as I walk, I can follow the squeaky interactions between an organic, talkative floor and a pair of shoes put in motion.

Around two-thirds into the space, I come across a curious sign, marking a much-desired rupture in the rather stable plot of shards, bones, clay pots, and arrowheads:

THIS EXHIBIT HAS BEEN
TEMPORARILY REMOVED AND WILL BE
RETURNED AS SOON AS POSSIBLE

A small laminated placard, standing by itself, as a stand-in for another displaced character. One may only assume that a certain urgency is implied, as if the temporary absence of the unknown object would create a void, a missing link in the object's task of telling the story of humankind's history on the planet. A void that could only be filled by acknowledging a gap in human perception. So what would normally be lodged between the stone chopping tool and the idol of the swimming reindeer? And what determined the display fate of the missing object? There is an inexhaustible list of external relations one could start to evoke: Was it a loan request? A restoration effort? A sudden invasion of woodworms?

Although some material contours of the missing object remain—notably a firm circular imprint left on the brown cloth lining the vitrine—one's attention is drawn to the informative sign sitting alongside it. The brightness of it certainly stands out from the overall muted tones, and one could only marvel at the idea that the sign is at least 6,500 years removed from its neighbors. But perhaps it is the thing itself, and especially what it tries to convey, that resonates with the missing object the most. The sign is a provocation in the face of the thing that is absent for the time being, and, rather than leaving an empty spot, it now inhabits the vitrine instead of that thing and comes to stand for the eradication itself. A sign for a missing sign, for a moment of indecision, that leaves space for a real-time simulation in the plot of an absent exhibition display.

<table>
<tr><td>(68)</td></tr>
<tr><td>**THIS WAY UP**</td></tr>
</table>

THIS WAY
THIS WAY
THIS WAY
THIS WAY
THIS WAY
THIS WAY
THIS WAY
THIS WAY
THIS WAY
THIS WAY
THIS WAY

UP
UP UP UP
UP UP UP UP UP
UP UP UP UP UP UP
UP UP UP UP UP UP UP UP

Above the grand entranceway, on the inside of the arch facing the exhibition, a large announcement board was installed. Measuring approximately 2 meters in width, it produced flickering and electrified displays of word combinations in red letters, changing at seemingly random intervals. In a far-reaching measure of context-responsiveness, the announcement board presented a different exhibition title whenever a change occurred in the makeup of the exhibition, responding to the number of visitors present, their individual backgrounds and levels of education, their movements in the exhibition space and interactions with the art objects, to mention just some of the parameters measured. Whether this happened through adaptive sensors interconnected with linguistic algorithms, or through the input of an all-observing staffed control room was hard to say, but it could nevertheless be said that the titling apparatus has great novelty value in providing tailor-made products to visitors of exhibitions.

TRANSPORT

Invisible choreographies often frame the time and space of an exhibition. Invisibility, however, always begs the question of the relativity of perspective and vantage point. On the subject of transport, the transitory patchwork activated when assembling dispersed actants in a given locale is most commonly felt on the level of the organizing body. To an exhibition visitor, transport often seems to have taken place without a single trace of the actual deed, of the endless streams of communication between the parties involved, among them transporting companies, artists, art handlers, and institutional hosts. Furthermore, the processes and workings of transportation remain undisputedly unseen to the extent that the tracks and traces it might convey—during arrival, unpacking, condition check, and removal—are cleared. From the viewpoint of the visitor's passing body, the transport process remains largely obscured and invisible; the exhibition has arrived and, well before any public viewing, the landing pad was removed.

In the joint venture of transportation, there is certainly an institutional carbon footprint that is formulated in correspondence with a number of stakeholders, among them galleries, museums, collectors, and packing and transportation companies. These stakeholders are amassed when the whereabouts of the different elements desired to enter into the frame of the exhibition are traced and delineated—from the robust marble installation stored in Peru, the Styrofoam object assumed to be in London, but actually held in storage at Minneapolis airport, to the performance troupe currently residing in Vienna.

From here, the cards are played accordingly: agreements are signed, alternatives are sought, and transportation companies submit their quotes. Multiple road movies—viewed through track-and-trace codes, retrospective invoices, and ETA speculations—start playing simultaneously. A pickup is arranged; a studio in Berlin is visited by a transportation company outsourced by yet another company. The distance traveled by each actant is measured by the number of working hours and fuel-tank refills needed to secure its passage. Other trajectories include the construction of two custom crates, an overnight stay in Dresden, one traveling in the convenience of the climate room, the other by boat and listed as "building material" instead of "art object."

From a well choreographed backstage shuffle in the cargo hold, to a sophisticated act of costume changes and layer shedding in the exhibition space. A cloaked object is first moved by forklift and then by trolley to its more or less decided location for display, and then it is gradually unveiled. The screws, the planks, the duct tape, and the Bubble Wrap all come off, a swift removal of the backing paper, pulleys are activated for the calibration of an exact placement, the pallet is dragged away, dusting and vacuum cleaning enacted, and, finally, it is marked on the spot and provided with a condition report. Neat. Welcome.

UNDERTONES

The reconfiguration of the institution's exterior wall forced a cascade of sounds, differing in duration and intensity, to leak through its newly implemented and porous threshold, and gradually trickle into the depths of its consecutive exhibition spaces. Indeed, it might well have been considered admirable to break through the hermetic façade by replacing segments of brick and mortar for large sheets of glass in order to reestablish the linkages between life on the street and the inner workings of the institution. However, by creating a heightened sense of inclusivity through visibility, the institution inadvertently welcomed an ambient mixture of noises, ranging from whistles, speech, and footsteps, to accelerating automobiles, bird sounds, and passing airplanes; a foundational layer of both more and less desired elements have now started to underpin the once quiet exhibition spaces.

In some ways, the exhibition space facing the street side became a sounding board for the world outside, a world not necessarily unknown but rather successfully abandoned in favor of the thick layers of material insulation that were long part of the modernist plan for optimized and neutral viewing conditions. From the first budget cuts to the casual withdrawal of the municipality's support, justified by the claim that the institution needed to open itself to the world, the institution now also had to face the world by letting it literally seep through its exterior walls.

The old modernist regime of white and cubical might find itself brokenhearted over the undesirable outside's permutation of its hermetic realms. Alternatively, the perspective might shift positively to consider the external stream of sounds as an active component of an exhibition. On this level, the institution could move toward the idea of being responsive to its wider environment and seek for its inscription in between the changing rhythm of its locality, becoming not so much a substance that remains stable over time, but rather a thing that subsists, that is enabled to last precisely because of those things that do not last.[1] May these small external references underpin and inform its programmatic fabric, and break through the walls, to unintentionally aid in the mobilization of an itinerant adaptation and transformation that becomes an unaccounted for, temporary part of the institution's inheritance. Art passes by like life, life passes by like art.

←

1 Paraphrased from: Bruno Latour, "No Transformation without Institution" (lecture, *Serpentine Transformation Marathon 2015*, Serpentine, London, October 17–18, 2015).

VIEWERS

How will this over-indebtedness to the viewing of exhibitions from an exclusively scopic, retinal perspective ever cease? This perceptual race of the senses, in which the scopic regime is somehow always chosen to restructure and digest the noise of the exhibition's proposed conceptual reality into seemingly coherent lumps of cognition. One could point out, quite obviously, that we are residing in the domains of visuality, that perception-making through the visual is our innovative currency, and that it should be encountered at face value. What could be said about vision and sight that would enable us to shift the dominant order of thinking about objects in an exhibition? Or perhaps the accompanying texts are to blame, with their suggested significations, hermeneutic circles, and descriptive generalizations that seem to correspond with and instruct what we see and shape our perception? Arguably, texts contribute to the preemption and restriction of the dimensionality of an object, which is so often considered to be too helpless and inadequate to communicate for itself, in turn chaining the viewers to an explanatory accompaniment.

There is no need whatsoever to meddle with the conception of the art objects that we take for granted as accountable perception-makers, or to solely invest in dematerialized practices from now on, but it is urgent to reconsider the prosthetics — organic and inorganic, internal to the body and external in the form of devices that come to our aid—employed in visual perception, problematic and impossible as that may be. Is it not that vision falls short, time and again, in providing an adequate and desired idea of cognitive perception in the context of an exhibition, in the sense that vision is a device for static although highly politicized acknowledgement: conducting mathematical measurements concerning sizes, dimensions, and compositions, and making observations that revolve around color, shape, and texture? What about those qualities and characteristics in objects that remain unseen, that are elusive, fleeting, and withdrawn from visual perception, a perception that is being pushed to the margins of reading surfaces, effects, and inter-dynamics, so that all the material ambiguities brought forward by the act of viewing are imposed and projected onto the "tacit" object and the intentionality of its maker? This concerns, in short, a question of indirect object knowledge through visual thought-inducement rather than an increasingly dimensional idea of trying to grasp and grapple with an object through the enabling of all the senses with the aim of access through encounter and experience.

How to resolve these disabling sensual incongruities, and to not let viewers find themselves standing in the bath water of phenomenology? Do we need to invent another object sign language for the blind that could already see, with great clarity and lucidity? Should we call for an assembly where ends can meet, "a parliament of things," to paraphrase the words of Bruno Latour, that strives toward the grounding of a common language among human and non-human entities?[1] Or should a general sense of pretense to the exhibition and its constituents be embraced, a necessary stretching and suspension of indecision, uncertainty, and not knowing, a much desired detour that sometimes comes in the shape of metaphors, mental extensions, and parallel references that saturate our viewing with indirectness and obliqueness? Or, could viewing be considered as the perceptual approximation of the object as a figment, an open-ended starting point rather than a closure, where viewing is not employed to see reason?

1   Bruno Latour, *We Have Never Been Modern*, trans. Catherine Porter (Cambridge: Harvard University Press, 1993), 142–5.

**VINYL
LETTERS**

The sheet of vinyl letters arrives in a tube one hour before the exhibition opens, and is applied as a wall essay with an ice scraper.[1]

1 The first draft of the wall essay provided by the curator was fought over with a marketer who considered the text to be so overly hermetic it would hardly appeal to the understanding of any audience member, with an additional request to reduce the word count from 400 to 150. In an aim to reach out, "the fleshed existence" was replaced by "the human body," and "to overcome the binary dialectics within advanced-capitalist society" by "economical ambiguity." A fresh-eyed senior had managed to "work" the text overnight, to land in the curator's mailbox the following morning. Upon disclosure, a battleground of annotations, corrections, and synonyms appeared, and matters quickly escalated after that: versions 5, 6, 7, 8_ed were born out of authorial pulling rather than an adversarial process, which commonly translates into a linear and chronologically written blurb, abandoning and reducing most of the textual possibilities, among them structural problems, unity and harmony, plot and story, time, textual effects, verisimilitude, narrative technique, characters, dialogue, setting(s), style, experience, and linguistic register.

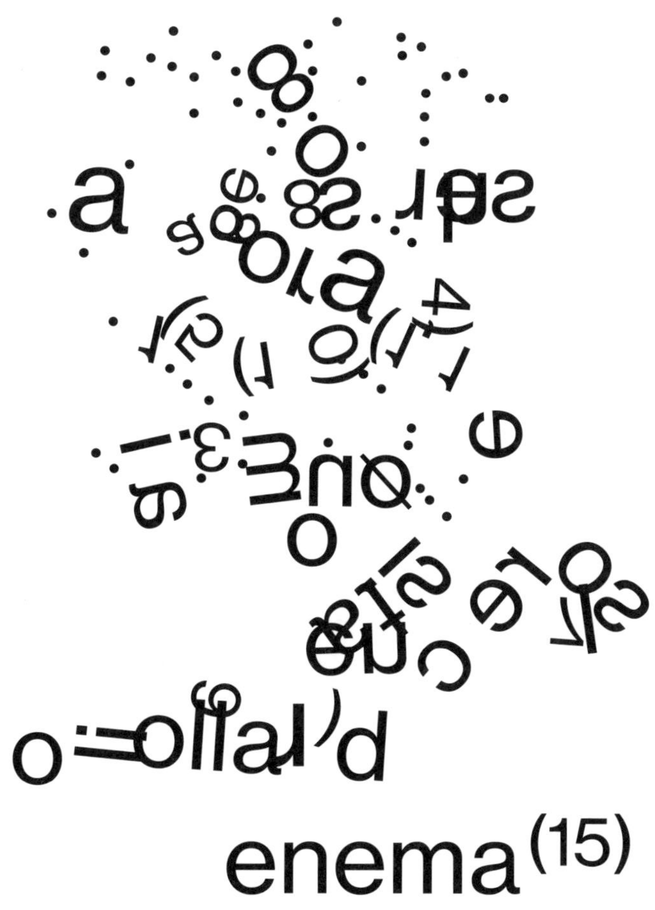

enema⁽¹⁵⁾

(74)
VISITORS

Visitors, dear visitors, you are shrouded in anonymity. Nevertheless, you are cordially invited ___ you are invited to discover ___ invited to purchase lunch ___ invited to become active participants ___ to select photographs ___ to become coauthors ___ to use the artists as vehicles for creating new wall paintings ___ you are invited to travel through the forest to interact with Duan—Visitors, dear visitors, you are welcome ___ welcome to explore ___ empowered to explore ___ empowered to envision hidden and parallel dimensions—Visitors can navigate the exhibition space using the handouts provided at the entrance ___ visitors can attend various events ___ can browse ___ can see and feel ___ visitors can come and have a chat ___ can participate in group discussions ___ can bring their own stories and points of view ___ visitors can have their portraits taken ___ visitors can give free rein to their anger by throwing virtual paving stones at websites—Visitors, dear visitors, you are encouraged… encouraged to read ___ to study ___ to donate ___ visitors are encouraged to sit and share with others ___ to reconsider the notion of territory ___ visitors are encouraged to lie down on the sculpture ___ encouraged to speak with Lerma—You are given the rare opportunity to meet important figures in a vibrant setting ___ the opportunity to talk with visual communications professionals—Visitors, dear visitors, you are allowed ___ you are allowed to interact ___ allowed to directly experience the works on display ___ make your own connections between objects ___ visitors are allowed to travel back in time and across the globe ___ allowed to engage with zine aficionados—Visitors are not allowed to enter due to the academic functioning of the institute—Visitors, dear visitors, you will ___ you will be accompanied on your journey through the exhibition ___ you will gain insight ___ you will be immersed ___ will witness ___ visitors will discover over five decades of creativity ___ will be confronted by immersive installations—The future will delight many visitors.[1]

---

1 **Material sourced from various e-flux-circulated press releases.**

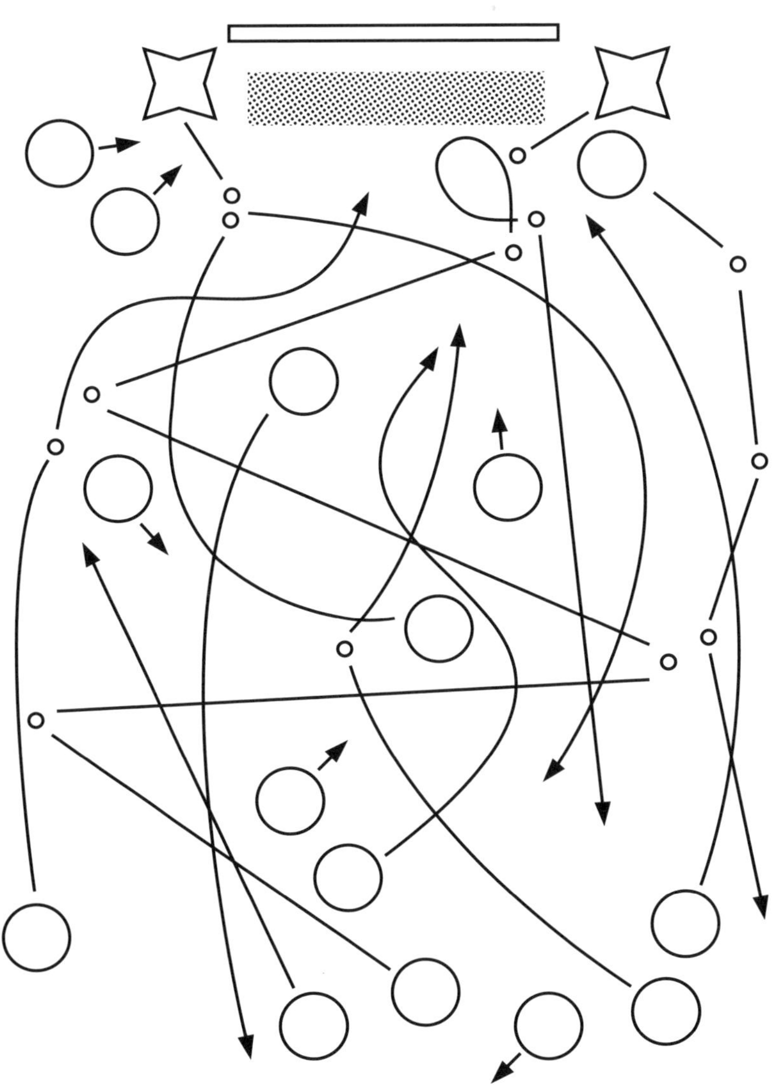

Choreography for two invigilators, fifteen visitors, and one painting

VITRINE

Please do not place drinks on the vitrines, as one might partially obscure their contents, leave circles on their surfaces, break the glass, or let fluids slip through the edges. Here we are facing a vitrine containing an assembly of various objects that have each undergone a cycle of objectification through the creation of two different temporalities: a vacuum and an external world.

There are no subjects here, neither is there a hint of the classic object-subject dichotomy, but merely objects framed differently and according to suggested and relative extremes and oppositions. The vitrine's state of temporal denial and mutual exclusiveness is marked by an unspoken and implied vow, one that is often pragmatic in nature: to take protective measures against the possible harm inflicted upon the state of the objects (and their corresponding value). But vitrines allocated to and built around objects cannot block out without shutting in, cannot secure without making security a way of life. Who is protecting themselves from whom? The objects, looking back at us, through the greasy mark left by a child's hand that wanted to grasp, but could not reach?

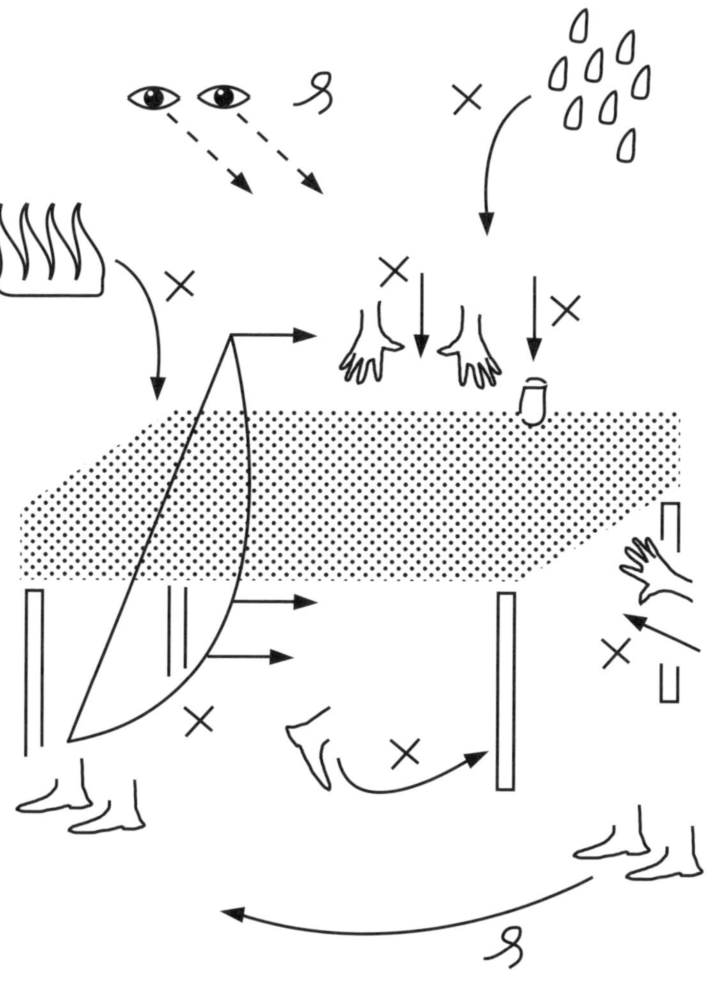

**WALLS
(MOVEABLE
AND
TEMPORAL)**

There is a lot to say about extending beyond walls, or going without walls altogether. In fact, decades of talking have passed with walls persisting as the demarcation of the boundary between private and public, interior and exterior. Walls that enclose make for convenient packages, and in the act of grouping and keeping occurrences within the territories they mark, they have come to stand for the assembly of matters infinitely more capacious and fleeting than their weighty, monolithic structures could possibly imply. This is not to undermine the structure of the wall, but to make a distinction between sensual walls that are physical, robust, and tangible, and real walls that reside in the space of concepts. From a human viewpoint, walls carry the burden of being our witnesses, of breathing and outliving our histories and the experiences lived within their confines. They become containers, enduring the ghosts of previous states. But who is to blame really? While we have been erecting and demolishing symbolic and hierarchical walls, making walls slide toward us in acts of protection and shelter, in establishing inclusion and exclusion mechanisms, and, on rare occasions, making windows where there were once walls, what is to be said about the walls within the walls of exhibition spaces that are intended to be moveable and temporary rather than lasting?

From rice paper, to plastered wooden skeletons and bricks and mortar, temporary walls form a tempo-spatial division within the exhibition space, constituting a structure that we could call an internal and dynamic circulation system. Nevertheless, this constellation-within-a-constellation still poses the question of how to approach the fixed architecture that surrounds the exhibition space: roof, permanent walls, floor, electricity, plumbing, and heating. How should we problematize the overarching structure from within so that it can adapt and redefine itself in order to be an adequate and provocative host? Here we could think of the temporary wall as a measure of consensus aiming to compensate for the static and rigid nature of the readily existing supports. A measure that obscures the "outside" world even further by turning a general overview into fragmented fields of

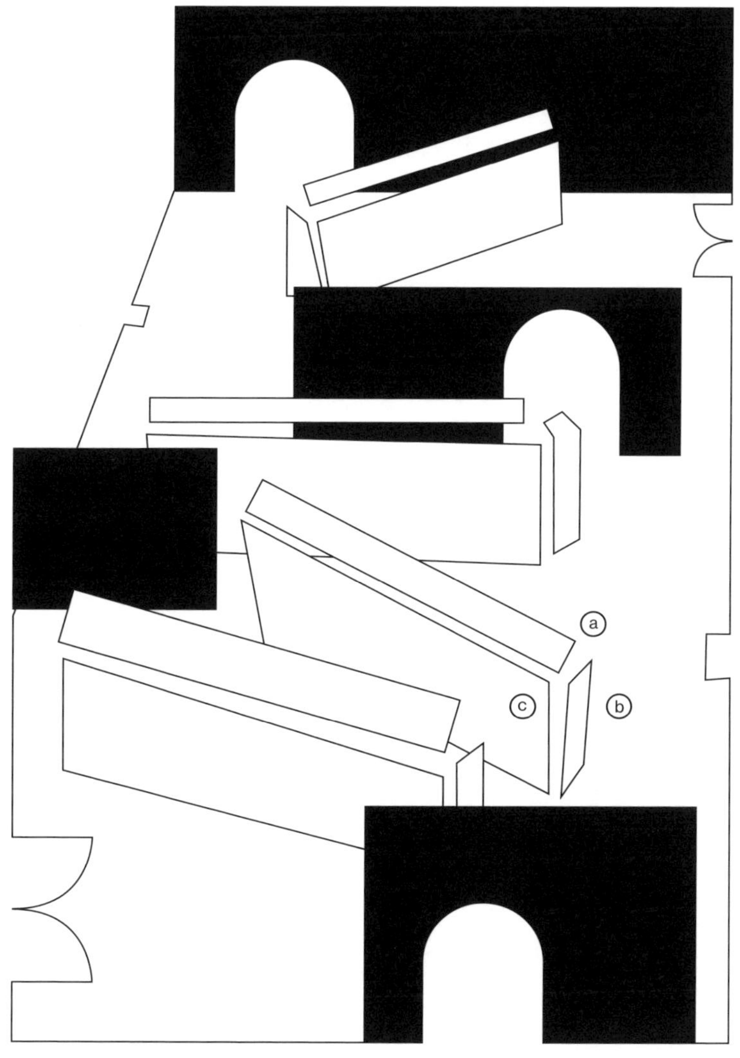
a
c
b

vision, into smaller plots and lumps of perceivable reality—structures of being that delineate and slice through structures of lived experience. As negative spaces and volumes of resistance, the consecutive placement of temporary walls punctuate rhythmical sequences, devise patterns of navigation, and perhaps even evoke a sense of folded time. However, the temporary wall as scenographic device might as well be mentally perforated and erased in the face of a human's movement through interlinking spaces, constantly converting concepts into objects, and objects back into concepts—though aided by the efforts of the temporary wall to mediate and enable frames of dedicated focus and brevity. Within this scenario we can fuse the projective potential of the temporary wall and the materials and objects it holds against itself—as backdrop—into the unstable ecology we call the exhibition, where volumes, real, lived, and symbolic, are erected and collapse.

77

WALL TEXT

In Luis Camnitzer's infamous work *This is a mirror. You are a written sentence* (1966–68), we are given an example of a text that approximates the exhibition wall text in its most defining shape: a self-contained, referential, and mirroring text that rather unfortunately triggers its readers to think about identification, context, and matters of fact, subtly bypassing the idea that the wall text, by its very nature, underscores the seeming inability of the exhibition and the objects it contains to communicate on their own terms. Were it not that the wall text's self-identifying and reflecting textual pointers are the abstracted outcome of yet another interpretive act, based on the institution's objective to provide a smooth introductory landing—a narrative bridging, connecting the visitor to the exhibition—the wall text would almost serve no purpose other than to reference itself in relation to the visitor. The wall text—introducing and explaining what an exhibition is concerned with and aiming to do—is at least at a double remove from a justified approach to the objects it pretends to enclose. As a container of words, the content of a wall text is therefore unmistakably bound to the space of description in which meaning is allocated to objects, but it is nevertheless held as a reliable sounding board for what can and is to be perceived. However, it is not the objects reflected in the text that are exhausted through the reductive capabilities of language, but rather it is the text closing in on itself. Additionally, as a linguistic construction, the wall text is spatially incapable of expressing both the potentiality and intentionality of the exhibition. As a result, we should allow ourselves a certain margin of leeway and vagueness as we move into these scripted and descriptive spaces. Let us externalize the wall text, and, similar to the cover of a book, we shall henceforth present it on an outside wall, preferably accompanied by a headline or quote provided by an unengaged author. Let us also treat the wall text as an idiosyncratic object in its own right, written in its language of choice and in its own handwriting.

WIRE (CABLE, EXTENSION CORD, AND STRING)

In the age of wire and string, we are taking our electricity sockets for granted as long as the streaming of content continues to be provided via the uninterrupted and "lively spark" ushered through interconnecting wires. Until the moment when a network that is constantly active but goes unseen is established, we distribute the sensible by means of physical connectedness, by chains of interlinking material parts that convey our texts, files, images, and sounds. Scopic circulation for scopic pleasure-seekers.

The exhibition landscape remains a battleground, constantly but unsuccessfully striving to negotiate a peace treaty between a seemingly endless stream of wire and the despotic powers of health and safety regulations. A conflict that is further informed by those objects of differing descent—a French projector, or an English media player—demanding to be attached to wires and extensions that have sprung from a similar origin. Here we see Capability Brown working toward an authentic experience that is utterly artificial by nature.[1] That is to say, if wires are to serve and support those objects that project and simulate, then why are they rejected visually? For what reasons does one invent plastic casings to make wires run straight, or wooden modules to hide clusters of sockets?

On the level of the exhibition, everything is a twice-performed performance in which the smooth video frame melts into the exhibition space and we only see the frame and that which it contains, not those parts that make the frame possible. This refusal of the supports leads toward what we might call the beautification of the exhibition space, aimed at securing optimized viewing conditions. In response, we might as well reverse the process and seek to go beyond the exhibition space as a neatly organized beautification area, and recover this conflict of fiberglass and copper wire in the key of the open circuit. What revolves around, within, and beyond the system resolves to be just as serious as the system itself.[2]

←

1 Lancelot Brown, also known as "Capability Brown," was an English landscape architect and gardener who is said to have seen opportunity for the plotting of artificial and constructed natural land-scapes where the situation provided to be so rough and wild others would have aban-doned the place. I always considered him to be a cardinal example of Enlightenment thinking in respect of both flattening lively matter and making it inert so as to carry out human projects.

2 This entry's title was in-spired by the book *The Age of Wire and String* (1995) by Ben Marcus. In the book we enter a reality that may indeed be based on and grounded in readily existing and knowable structures of being and living, but it manages to introduce a whole new system of references and destabilized or-ders, where objects acquire different mean-ings and applications, and where humans engage in all sorts of primordial rites and object relations.

We Need to Talk About Dolphins

By Timotheus Vermeulen

In the spirit and in honor of Niekolaas Johannes Lekkerkerk's poetic and episodic study of the museological apparatus—if "apparatus" is indeed the right word—I thought I, too, would offer here a series of five loosely connected thoughts with respect to Lekkerkerk's study—as opposed to a single, linear argument. Some of these observations pertain directly to Lekkerkerk's entries, but there are also notes that, well, take a rather more roundabout approach to the matter at hand. Each of my observations, however, manifest in their own way as attempts to think through and think with the questions that the text poses: What is the relationship between an exhibition and its space? Or between an exhibition and its objects? Are exhibitions always already ideological? Can we think matter without thinking meaning? To be sure, my attempts are inevitably and without exception, failures. I would like to think that they are failures because the questions are either impossible to answer or in any case too difficult (for me) to answer in the space I have available here; but I hope that in the process of articulating these failures, something is (here comes the cliché) nonetheless achieved, something that I think Lekkerkerk's book achieves as well: a crystallization, in the sense not of clarity but of the prism, in offering numerous perspectives of how we may go about beginning to tackle these questions.

Anthropocentrism and Anthropomorphism

In 2014 I conducted an interview with Rosi Braidotti for *frieze*. Toward the end of our conversation, she said the following, which has stuck with me since and with which I agree wholeheartedly:

> *You can be a posthumanist and post-anthropocentric thinker. In fact, in advanced capitalism, in which the human species is but one of the marketable species, we are all already post-anthropocentric. But I don't think we can leap out of our anthropomorphism by will. We can't. We always imagine from our own bodies—and why should we, considering that we still live on a planet populated by humanoids who think of themselves as humans, in different ways, with different points of reference? Our very embodiment is a limit, as well as a threshold; our flesh is framed by the morphology of the human body, it is also always already sexed and hence differentiated.*[1]

What resonates with me in Braidotti's argument is this: we can think about things, and we can think about the agency of things, about what things do and about what things want, and we can even think about what things are or might be within their own terms, and we can speculate on Schrodinger's cat, for instance, through algorithms and so much more; but it is always us, humans—you, me, others—thinking these thoughts and affects. This is not to say that I do not think we should, in order to extend philosophy as a program, as Reza Negarestani has so eloquently put it, speculate about things—what they do and want and are and could be—but I do feel it is important to understand that this speculation is just that, speculation, that is, a fiction, in the same sense that so much of the natural sciences and mathematics are fictional, calculating with variables in order to hypothesize about what reality may be. I imagine that depending on who is reading this, you either find this self-evident or incredibly ignorant; but it seems to me important to reconsider this debate, especially, and presumably

[1]
Timotheus Vermeulen and Rosi Braidotti, "Borrowed Energy,"
frieze 165 (2014): 130–3.

unpopularly, in light of recalling Immaanuel Kant's *Critique of Judgment* and his essays on history, Leibniz, and especially the long-forgotten Hans Vaihinger and his philosophy of the as-if.

To Parallelize

The purpose of this book as I understand it is threefold. Its two structuring functions—literally, in the sense that they structure the format of the book—are to read the museological apparatus—the nuts and bolts of the act of displaying, of showcasing art in a gallery, ranging from the vitrine to wires to an art handler to pedestals to oxygen to marketing tools (but not, somewhat surprisingly, unskilled labor or vacuum cleaners or sponges or painters or waste services)—as if it were a language, an alphabet; and to reflect on the extent to which this language, this alphabet, is context specific, can be put together differently and to different effects in other contexts, i.e., not-art contexts (in the sense that in the museological context wires plus pedestal plus television set signifies one phenomenon, "s" plus "e" plus "e" makes "see," whereas in another situation, for example an electronics store or a shanty town, it invokes another ("buy" or "status" or "community")). The book's author, the talented young curator Lekkerkerk, is keen to stress from the get-go that there is a third function, one which opposes the other two, or rather still undermines them, dissolves the structure they compose. As Lekkerkerk notes, he might treat "exhibition-making" as "a form of spatial writing by means of objects," but he simultaneously seeks to unshackle these objects not only from their particular signifying chains but from "linguistic, semiotic, and symbolic" signification more generally; that is to say, in more popular lingo, he seeks to speculate about their "thingness," to devise here, in his own words, an "ontico-fictional study." Though I feel the first two goals—theorizing exhibition making as spatial writing and relativizing the correlation between words and meanings—are achieved, the third—speculation about their "thingness," about what they "are"—I guess, is suspended, or indeed, as Jacques Derrida might have remarked (in the margin of the text), infinitely postponed, eternally pushed further afield by this relationship and that interaction and so on. Lekkerkerk sets out to territorialize and de-territorialize the museological domain without re-territorializing it. What he manages in contrast, through his anecdotes and reveries and language games, is to territorialize, de-territorialize, and what we might call, following Robert Musil, "parallelize," demonstrating not so much all that one thing "can be" than every*thing* it might become for something or someone or somewhere or sometime else—what Musil talks about when he talks about "a sense of possibility."[2] I would certainly not call this suspension of an apprehension of things as they are a failure, however, for even though it does not show us the face of the *Ding-an-Sich*, it does envisage, from multiple sides, its contours (like a 3D or 4D version of the cave metaphor).

Space

It is fair to say, I guess, that spatial theory, wittingly and unwittingly, is divided into two camps (there might be more, there might indeed, be tens of camps, the Leibnizians and Deleuzians and Whiteheadians and so on and forth, but for argument's sake, let's not overly *Game of Thrones* this debate here): the De Certeauans and the Lefebvrians. The former believe that space is always *espacement*, spatialization: the putting into action of a given set of parameters, which they call "places." From the looks of it, Lekkerkerk associates himself with this camp, at least initially: the exhibition is the spatialization of a series of objects and/or agents, i.e., places, that exist—that "are"—independently (but not necessarily outside of ideology). Indeed, Lekkerkerk even adopts the metaphor the De Certeauans tend to use: that of language, grammar, the alphabet, in which space is like the word when it is spoken. Or, in Michel de Certeau's famous phrase: "space is a practiced place."

As I have written elsewhere, I am sympathetic to the ideas of the second camp, that of the Lefebvrians. For the Lefebvrians, space is less the performance of a script than it is a negotiation between systemic or social (the ideas of the bankers and bureaucrats and architects), affective (memories,

2
Robert Musil, *The Man Without Qualities*
(London: Picador, [1978] 1997), 10–13.

dreams, anxiety attacks), and performative and/or material forces (your body's behavior), or, in Lefebvrian terms: conceived, lived, and perceived space. Where for De Certeauans, space is either an affirmation or a negation of the script, for Lefebvrians, space is a much more open-ended improvisation. That does not mean that there is not a power play at work here, that the systemic force might be stronger depending on the nature of the society or community producing the space, but things are not, not necessarily at least, written in stone. In other words, for the De Certeauans space performs ideology in its entirety; for the Lefebvrians, space *is* ideological, is always already ideological, but not necessarily totally (or not in a coherent, unified way). Were we to approach the museological apparatus along these lines, we might still further broaden and nuance Lekkerkerk's project, opening up questions about the nature of the rooms and the objects and the agents in different realms of consideration. What is the space produced by copper wire? How might an arrow painted onto the floor (a conceived space, to be sure) link up with perceived and lived spaces? What forces propel the art handler? Lekkerkerk talks about the "ecology" of the exhibition space, which seems an apt term: For what kind of universe is this, by what forces is it ruled? What is possible and what is impossible? What is likely and unlikely? What is beneficial and detrimental?

Talking with Dolphins

A while back I read an article about talking dolphins. I do not remember where it was published. I doubt it was the most reliable of sources. I noticed it because it was linked on social media with some frequency. In any case, the article said, or said something along the lines of, that researchers had cracked the language of dolphins. They had put microphones in the water, and had located the echoes of the pitches and squeaks dolphins let out, or whatever sound it is that dolphins make. The researchers had transcribed these points of sonic contact and found, to their surprise, or so it was alleged, that together they looked like images—figurative images, images that could be understood by humans, images, indeed, that resembled how, since the days of the cave paintings but more still since the Renaissance, with its distinct rules of perspective, we humans conceive of images. If you do not believe me, look it up: the article shows a photograph of a dolphin and a dude in the water alongside the accompanying sonograph, which depicts that guy as a stick figure.

Obviously, I have no clue whether the story is true. I doubt it, to be honest, but since I am not a marine biologist it would be disingenuous for me to make any claims about its veracity. Judging from what other people have said, however, specialists in the field (I realize that specialists are not all too popular these days, Foucaulted to the margin of the debate, stitched shut as mouthpieces for this or that ideology, but to my mind, they are still our best bet in most scenarios), it appears to be utter nonsense. In any case, it does not matter, for me, whether this story is true or false. What interests me is the attention the story received, in other media, on Facebook, from friends: the jubilation, the hosannas, the "you-see-I-told-you-sos." People were, if only for a moment, extremely excited by the possibility that dolphins talked in a language we could fathom. To me, this exhilaration suggests two things: first, there is a human desire, perhaps innate but at least prevalent today, for the world to be meaningful in and of itself beyond human interference, a kind of alter- or posthumanism; and second, this posthuman meaning should, somehow, be understandable to humans, or rather still, should be translatable, reducible, to human discourse (the whole modernist "the-world-is-a-puzzle-that-fits" shtick, the same line that produces God particles and all that stuff). Perhaps, I guess, there is a third implication here, if pushed: humans would love interspecies interaction but especially if it is on their own, that is, the human's own terms, in spite, or maybe also because, of all the ontological, epistemological, and above all ethical quandaries that would raise (i.e., we are the ones putting the puzzle together). To put it differently, if we talk about posthumanism, do we not also always talk about everything that is not human—for whatever reason, whether it is fatigue with centuries of philosophy focusing solely on the human, or a real sense that without this change of point of view we lose the "outside" world—precisely so as to reassert ourselves as humans, a sort of contemporary orientalism or exoticism, this time not directed to human others but to nonhuman others? I realize this assertion is based on next to nothing, to a handful of reactions to a viral news feed, but I have a hunch it is not a single incident. Either way, it seems to me important to take into consideration why, exactly, we are so interested in the non-human: Why do we care about the other lives of copper wire and the vitrines and television sets, handkerchiefs and tender buttons? What is in it, for us?

Tender Buttons

I assume Lekkerkerk's project was inspired, at least to some extent, by Gertrude Stein's *Tender Buttons* (1914), a series of more and less poetic reflections on objects and rooms, on stuff and spaces, that may or may not have been realist and/or symbolic (you know, the whole tender, ahem, "buttons" you learn about in school). There is another contemplation of the most tender of buttons I would like to infer here: in *The Weltanschauung as an Ersatz Gestalt,* a brilliant and too little-known study of matter and meaning, Jan Turnovsky uses the buttons as a case study in ideology and historical necessity:

> *They tell us that every button has de facto only two holes which were already there before the button. But somebody tries to sell us four pretty holes in the most ornamental — though seemingly ornamentless — button. [And] [s]omebody else explain[s] to us why buttons with ornaments were abandoned, or how to sew on our buttons in the right or left way.*[3]

Turnovsky illustrates his argument with a series of splendid black-and-white drawings of buttons each attached to an invisible jacket or shirt in a different manner: there is the independent button without strings and the schizophrenic button with the string looping through the holes unevenly; the clerical button with its string in a cross and an egalitarian button, its top holes linked in the exact same way as its bottom holes; the pacificist button with the string tied like the peace symbol; and the obscene button, the eccentric and the jazzy and the frustrated and the tectonic and the

3

Jan Turnovsky,
***The Weltanschauung as an Ersatz Gestalt. Eine Happy-open-end-
environmental-design-science-fiction-image-story,*** eds. Eva Guttmann, Gabriele Kaiser,
and Claudia Mazanek (Zurich: Park Books, 2016), 75.

decadent and so on. It is a remarkable sight. What interests me here is what interests me about the distinction between the De Certeauans and the Lefebvrians: the extent to which, and the manner in which, matter and meaning correlate and/or can be studied independently from one another. Is Turnovsky's button with two holes the ideological *idée fixe* without which the ornamentalization, that is to say, this particular expression of creativity, is not conceivable, not the exact same thing as the exhibition apparatus? Should we not wait to ask what the wires, or the pedestal, or the vitrines, are until we understand what they can and cannot mean and, especially, be seen to be within the universe at hand and that universe's history—a retracing of steps, an unraveling of the spool, a dismantling of the wall? For me, this is where Lekkerkerk's study hits the—no pun intended—nail on the head: together, the entries retrace, unravel, disman-tle, with each step, ball of wool, or brick looking at the other concoctions that might have been possible, a science fiction not of the future, if you will, but of the past.

Biographies

Sonia Dominguez
(b. 1988, CH) works as a freelance graphic designer. She graduated in visual communication from HEAD – Genève (Geneva University of Art and Design). In 2012, she cofounded her first studio and since then she has collaborated with different clients, especially in the fields of art and culture. Her interest in creating and composing books led her to work on different editorial projects, in, among other places, Switzerland, the Netherlands, and Belgium. In parallel, she employs a multidisciplinary approach in developing visual identities and digital structures, gaining a broader perspective on her graphic practice through the application of her digital skills. She has collaborated with Niekolaas Johannes Lekkerkek on various projects, for example in 2014 with the poster for the group exhibition "John Smith, the Posthuman" at the Bonnefantenmuseum, Maastricht (cocurated with Sally Müller), and in 2011 with the visual identity for The Office for Curating.

Tim Hollander
(b. 1987, NL) works as an artist and incidental curator. He graduated with a bachelor of fine arts from the Hogeschool voor de Kunsten in Utrecht in 2014, and won the Jan Zumbrink Prijs in the process. Between 2016 and 2017 he was a resident at the Van Eyck Academy in Maastricht. Recent exhibitions include the self-curated group exhibition "When Attitudes Become Multiform" at the Van Eyck, Maastricht (2017); the solo exhibitions "Institutional Soup" and "Conceptual Soup" at Art Rotterdam and P/////AKT, Amsterdam respectively (2016); and the solo exhibition "Curating the Collection (1992–2014)" at Kunsthal Rotterdam (2015). He also curated and exhibited in the exhibition "Reading Between Not-straight Lines" at Academiegalerie, Utrecht (2015) and participated in various group exhibitions including "The Museum of Unconditional Surrender" at TENT, Rotterdam (2015), curated by Niekolaas Johannes Lekkerkerk.

Niekolaas Johannes Lekkerkerk (b. 1988, NL) works as a curator and a writer. In September 2012 he founded The Office for Curating, which is currently based in Rotterdam. In parallel he has maintained different institutional affiliations, recently as curatorial fellow at TENT, Rotterdam (2015–16) and as artistic director of Poppositions, Brussels (2017–18). Recent exhibition projects include: the duo-exhibition "Homestead of Dilution" with Domenico Mangano and Marieke van Rooy at Nomas Foundation, Rome (2017); the group exhibitions "Tradition Doesn't Graduate" at KOMPLOT, Brussels, and "Spending Quality Time With My Quantified Self" at TENT, Rotterdam (both 2016); the solo exhibition "Sliding under Traces" with Paul Geelen at A Tale of a Tub, Rotterdam (2016); "The Earthbound," a screening series that took place at Cannonball, Miami (2015); the group exhibition "The Museum of Unconditional Surrender" at TENT, Rotterdam (2015); the group exhibition "Percussive Hunter" at Akbank Sanat, Istanbul (2015); as well as the group exhibition "John Smith, the Posthuman" at the Bonnefantenmuseum, Maastricht (2014). In 2012 he was the recipient of the inaugural NEON Curatorial Award from Whitechapel Gallery, London, in recognition of his fiction- and literature-based approach to curating. In 2014 he won the Akbank Sanat International Curator Competition.

Publication Services is a text and image editing collective of shifting proportions. It was founded in 2016 while mixing drinks on a rooftop in downtown Cairo.

Timotheus Vermeulen is associate professor in media, culture, and society at the University of Oslo. He has written extensively about contemporary culture and aesthetics, in particular film and television. His latest book *Metamodernism: Historicity, Affect, and Depth after Postmodernism* (Rowman & Littlefield, 2017), was co-edited with Robin van den Akker and Alison Gibbons.

Acknowledgements

Niekolaas Johannes Lekkerkerk would like to thank the contributors and collaborators who are part of this book, Nico de Oliveira for triggering the author's initial curiosity for the world of exhibitions, Gudrun Bott and Marcus Lütkemeyer for facilitating an initial writing period between June and December 2014 at Schloss Ringenberg, Germany, Mariette Dölle and the staff at TENT, Rotterdam, for hosting the exhibition "The Museum of Unconditional Surrender" (2015) that was a testing ground for the ideas articulated in this book, Robert Lekkerkerk and Sanny Kastelein, Imco van Gent, Nina Swaep, and Rianne Groen for their ongoing encouragement, and Sanne Goudriaan for all her love and support.

Colophon

Onomatopee 141

**The Standard Book
of Noun-Verb
Exhibition Grammar**
by Niekolaas Johannes Lekkerkerk

ISBN 978-94-91677-74-8

This book was made possible
with the support of:
• Mondriaan Fund
• Creative Industries Fund NL

First edition of 1,100 copies

M mondriaan
fund

**creative industries
fund NL**

Published by
Onomatopee
Willemstraat 27
5611 HB Eindhoven
The Netherlands
info@onomatopee.net

Edited by
Publication Services

Text contribution by
Timotheus Vermeulen

Drawings by
Tim Hollander

Designed by
Sonia Dominguez

Proofread by
Publication Services

Project managed by
Sanne Goudriaan

Printed by
Art Libro / Drukkerij Roelofs

Take the exhibition as a sentence, identify the object and subject of the sentence. Find the third term – the abject – which is excluded by the split between object and subject, but which somehow messes with the difference.